The Central Panel System for Administrative Law Judges:

A Survey of Seven States

The Central Panel System for Administrative Law Judges:

A Survey of Seven States

Malcolm C. Rich
Wayne E. Brucar

American Judicature Society
Chicago
University Publications of America, Inc.
Frederick, Maryland

Sponsorship of this project by the American Judicature Society signifies that the matter studied is regarded as important and that the study is thought to be valuable and responsible. The analyses, conclusions, and opinions expressed are the authors' and not necessarily those of the Society, its officers, members, or others associated with the organization. The assistance of the Administrative Conference of the U.S. in this project is gratefully acknowledged.

American Judicature Society
200 West Monroe Street
Suite 1606
Chicago, Illinois 60606
(312) 558-6900

Table of Contents

Preface   vii

1   Introduction   1

2   The Central Panel Within the Administrative Process   7

3   The Process of Implementation   17

4   The Structure of Central Panels   27

5   The Role of the Administrative Law Judge Within the
    Central Panel   45

6   The Hearing Process and the Central Panel   67

7   Summary and Conclusion   83

Appendices   87
A   Breakdown of Mean Responses by State of Employment   89
B   Other Types of Cases Reported/Heard by Central Panel ALJs   94

Bibliography   95

About the Authors   99

List of Tables

3-1   Central Panel Systems: Methods of Funding   24

4-1   Summary of Key Features of Central Panel Systems   28

4-2   Jurisdiction of Seven Central Panel Systems   29

4-3   Central Panel Operations: Reported Number of Contested Cases
      Filed and Number of ALJs   32

4-4   Central Panel Systems: Budgets   33

4-5   Central Panels: Responsibilities   34

4-6   How Cases Reach the Central Panels for Hearing   35

4-7   Directors' Profiles: A Sampling of Duties   36

4-8   Directors' Profile: Official Title   37

4-9   Directors' Profile: Qualifications   37

4-10   Directors' Profile: Appointment   38

4-11   Directors' Profile: Term of Office   39

4-12   Directors' Profile: Formal Methods of Evaluation
       and Removal   39

5-1   Administrative Law Judges' Profile: Official Title   51

5-2   Administrative Law Judges' Profile: Qualifications   51

5-3   Administrative Law Judges' Profile: How ALJs Said
       They Were Recruited   52

5-4   Administrative Law Judges' Profile: Selection Process   53

5-5   Selected Characteristics of Central Panel ALJ Respondents   55

5-6   Selected Characteristics of Central Panel ALJ Respondents
       by State   56

5-7   Administrative Law Judges' Profile: Term of Office
       and Removal Provisions   58

5-8   Administrative Law Judges' Profile: Evaluation   59

5-9   Administrative Law Judges' Profile: Promotion and
       Salary Decisions   60

5-10   Viewpoints of Central Panel ALJ Respondents on Evaluation
       and Expertise   61

5-11   Work-Related Attitudes of Central Panel ALJ Respondents
       By State   61

5-12   Work-Related Viewpoints of Central Panel ALJ Respondents   62

5-13   Work-Related Attitudes of Central Panel ALJ Respondents
       By State   63

5-14   How Administrative Law Judges are Assigned: Case by Case or to One Agency for an Extended Time Period   63

5-15   Administrative Law Judge Assignment: Expertise   64

6-1   Work-Related Activities of Central Panel ALJ Respondents   72

6-2   Reported Work-Related Activities of Central Panel ALJs   73

6-3   Reported Resources Available to Central Panel ALJs   74

6-4   Hearing Process: Rules of Procedure   75

6-5   Hearing-Related Activities: Are Hearings Public, Are Hearings Recorded, and Is There a Right to Counsel?   76

6-6   Types of Cases Heard by Central Panel Administrative Law Judges   76

6-7   Patterns in Types of Cases Heard Frequently by Central Panel ALJ Respondents   77

6-8   Hearing-Related Reported Activities of Central Panel ALJs   78

6-9   Hearing Process: Form of Administrative Law Judge Decision   79

6-10   Hearing Process: Can Litigants See the ALJ's Decision Before the Agency Issues its Final Order   80

6-11   Hearing Process: Is ALJ Decision Final or Recommended?   80

6-12   Hearing Process: The Extent to which Agencies Accept ALJ Decisions   81

6-13   Central Panel Agencies: How Are ALJ Decisions Cataloged?   81

Preface

Administrative Law Judges (ALJs) are major figures in America's justice system. There are more than 4000 state and federal ALJs, serving about 30 federal agencies and as many as 100 in each state. The life of nearly everyone is affected in some way by decisions rendered by these administrative judges, yet the administrative system of justice has only recently begun to receive the attention that it deserves. Federal ALJs have been the subject of many articles in recent years—from academic journals to newspapers, but state administrative judges have remained a "hidden judiciary." This is the case despite the fact that many of the same issues of efficiency and fairness that affect the federal system now affect the states, too, and many of them are working to resolve these issues in a new way.

The approach seven states have implemented is the central panel system, in which administrative law judges are not employed by the agencies whose cases they hear but by a distinct agency created solely to manage them. Another state, Washington, enacted enabling legislation for its central panel in late 1981 and New York City has utilized a central panel system since 1979.

The central panel system is a framework that increases the "judicialization" of the state administrative law process by seeking to keep ALJs separate from the agencies they serve, and to thereby ensure fair, high caliber decisionmaking. The purpose of this monograph is to highlight the central panel system and to examine the ways each of seven states has adapted this approach to its unique political and economic environment.

This monograph is part of a three-pronged approach to examining the central panel system. On May 8, 1981, a workshop was held in Chicago to provide a forum for exchange of information among state and federal ALJs and researchers doing work in the administrative law area. Cosponsored by the American Judicature Society and the Administrative Conference of the U.S., the workshop allowed its participants to discuss candidly the similarities and differences between the state and federal adjudicative systems, and to consider the strengths and weaknesses of central panel systems.

The second prong was the November 1981 issue of *Judicature* which was devoted to the administrative law process. The articles, written by both practitioners and researchers, provided an overview of the central panel approach and a specific examiniation as to how particular central panel systems operate.

The third prong is this monograph, which elaborates upon how the central panel approaches in seven states fit into the administrative system of justice. The first chapter introduces the role of the administrative law judges—and how that role is changed by the addition of a central panel approach. In Chapter 2, we discuss the different ways in which the administrative process functions in the federal and state systems. We then discuss the major characteristics of the central panel—including proposed advantages and disadvantages. We identify, in Chapter 3, some of the opponents and proponents of the central panels in our seven states—and why they took their positions. We also discuss the ways in which the panels were implemented—and the resulting consequences. Finally, we explore the methods in which the central panel approach changes the way states pay for hearings.

The remainder of the monograph looks at the specific operating procedures and policies in the seven states. Chapter 4 focuses on the similarities and differences in the ways central panel agencies are structured. In Chapter 5, we look at the structure of the ALJ role within the central panel, the ways in which ALJs are recruited, selected, and evaluated in state systems, and the work-related viewpoints that central panel ALJs expressed to us concerning their role. Chapter 6 examines the role of the central panel ALJ in the hearing process—the day-to-day work behavior of central panel ALJs. We offer a summary and our conclusions in Chapter 7.

The authors wish to thank the Administrative Conference of the U.S. for its support of this monograph as well as the May 1981 workshop on central panel systems. The Conference, an independent federal agency, was established in 1968 to recommend improvements on the administrative procedures followed by federal departments and agencies. In recognition of innovations in state administrative procedure (and their potential application to the federal system), the Conference has begun to support research and workshops on administrative law issues facing the states.

We also wish to thank Mr. Jeff Lubbers, Senior Staff Attorney at the Administrative Conference, and Mr. L. Harold Levinson, Professor of Law at Vanderbilt University, for their helpful comments and suggestions. Another individual we wish to thank is Mr. Victor Rosenblum, Professor of Law and Political Science at Northwestern University, who provided us the benefits of his extensive knowledge of administrative law as well as his insightful and thoughtful views regarding the roles of administrative law judges. Finally, the authors thank Mr. Lance Reed for his research assistance.

The central panel represents an organizational innovation its proponents say will improve the administration of justice. Its opponents say it is a step toward reducing the discretion of administrative agencies and, thus, toward reducing the effectiveness of the administrative process. This monograph seeks to highlight the major operating procedures and policies of existing central panels so as to allow a better informed assessment of this new approach.

The authors hope that this work will spur other researchers and practitioners to begin work into the study of state administrative adjudication as well as into the federal administrative process. These areas require thoughtful analysis, for while state and federal agencies are prime targets for budget-cutting, their actions continue to affect the quality of life. And, as a critical component of agency processes, it is the ALJs who often establish state and national policies. It is, therefore, imperative that not only the efficiency, integrity, and impartiality of the administrative judiciary not be endangered by budget-cutting measures, but that these objectives of administrative justice be enhanced.

1
Introduction

The administrative process was originally designed to serve as an alternative to court action in complex economic and scientific matters. This process has, for nearly a century, helped establish public policy while providing administrative procedures to protect against perceived abuses of power by governmental agencies. Proponents of this process claim that social complexities require technical expertise and swift decisionmaking that formal court action cannot deliver.[1] Most states and the federal government have established increasingly formalized, quasi-judicial proceedings for rulemaking and to hear specific regulatory and social welfare cases.

Critics, however, have decried the system as "administrative absolutism," a system that affects the lives of every citizen but is not held sufficiently accountable for its actions—and called for judicial review of agency action. In fact, the courts since the 1930s have played a large role in reviewing administrative decisions and in dictating standards under which agencies must operate.

Other critics of the administrative process focus their attention on the procedures used by agencies. Some charge that government uses these agencies to deprive citizens of their rights and they call for more due process guarantees for administrative litigants.[2] Practitioners have openly questioned whether the administrative hearing officer—who is usually an agency employee—can provide a fair hearing.[3]

The Role of the Administrative Law Judge

Formalizing the procedural aspects of administrative adjudication was a major step toward what we call the judicialization of the administrative hearing process, which makes it more closely resemble the independent model of our general jurisdiction courts. A critical component in this evolution has been the administrative law judges (ALJs) who serve about 30 federal agencies and as many as 100 in each state, resolving often complex disputes between agencies and the public. Although their rulings are "initial decisions" subject to review, in practice most become the final agency ruling; what they decide thus affects the daily lives of nearly everyone.

Administrative judges, because virtually every aspect of adjudication is related to their role, have often been a part of efforts to respond to the criticisms of administrative agencies. Federal and state governments have attempted to safeguard due process rights and improve administrative effectiveness by utilizing ALJs in different ways. One way in which these approaches differ is the extent to which ALJs are separated from administrative agencies. In many states, the hearing officer remains a tightly supervised employee of the agency for which he or she hears cases. Agencies usually have control over hiring, firing, and disciplining ALJs.

The federal approach is to allow the ALJ to remain an employee of a particular agency but to provide career appointment (tenure until retirement) and to give responsibility for the compensation and discipline of ALJs to bodies separate from the agencies (U.S. Office of Personnel Management and the Merit Systems Protection Board, respectively). A new approach which separates ALJs from agencies even further is the central panel system. Seven states have removed ALJs from particular agencies and placed them within an independent agency, thus creating a central pool or central panel of ALJs. It is an experiment in administrative adjudication that with one exception began only in the last decade. An eighth state, Washington, has enacted enabling legislation for a central panel[4] and New York City has utilized a central panel of hearing officers since 1979. The central panel approach is designed to make the ALJ more independent of agency influence and is, thus, a step toward the judicialization of the administrative process.

Another distinction between the central panel and federal system is the amount of information available about each. Although the federal administrative process has become a popular topic for descriptive studies, the central panel system (and, indeed, state adjudication in general) remains little explored. It is the goal of this monograph to examine the central panel approach so that we can compare the new approach to the federal system and discern the differences in the ALJ's role in the central panel states: California, Colorado, Florida, Massachusetts, Minnesota, New Jersey and Tennessee. To structure our study, we will divide it into five major topics which focus on different aspects of central panel systems and the role of the ALJ in those systems.

1. The strengths and weaknesses of the central panel approach in light of the purposes of the administrative process

Over the last century, there has been an ongoing debate concerning the extent to which hearing officers should be separated from the agency for which they hear cases. How could the hearing officer provide the independent decisionmaking critical to a judicial-like system if he or she were employed by the agency? Would a system that allowed the hearing officer to be independent of the agency be counterproductive to the concept of administrative policymaking? Because of the importance of the ALJ to the system, these questions have been at the heart of changes made since the 1930s. Through the Administrative Procedure Act of 1946,[5] the federal government recognized a need for ALJ independence. Through the central panel system, seven states have done the same. But while both changes have resulted in a separation of hearing officers from agencies, each has achieved this end in a different way. We will, in Chapter 2, delineate proposed advantages and disadvantages of these approaches.

2. The problems of implementing a central panel

Since any major structural change will often encounter resistance, it was no surprise to find opposition when central panel systems were operationalized in states where hearing officers had been part of the agencies for decades. While we did not focus our efforts in this area, in Chapter 3 we sought to identify the proponents and opponents of the legislation which created the central panels, the methods used by the two sides, and the purposes of these actions.

The concept of a central panel in each state has been shaped by the political process. The current structures of the systems reflect the compromises that were made during the legislative battles preceding their enactment—and the resistance that followed. To understand why the systems have the form they do, it is important to examine the implementation process, including resistance at the legislative and post-legislative periods.

Another aspect of implementing an innovation involves new methods of funding and administrative cost controls. Fiscal matters were often important to legislators considering central pools—and continue to be of prime importance in states considering new adjudicative systems.[6] We have identified the ways in which seven states fund their central panel systems, and through interviews with the pools' directors we learned how the type of funding can affect daily operations and relationships between the central pools and agency officials.

3. The structure and operation of the central panel systems

Previous research has described central panels from the vantage of their enabling statutes, the state administrative procedure acts. Our goal in Chapter 4 is to provide information concerning the day-to-day workings of central panels that statutory surveys cannot provide. Specifically, we profiled the central panel directors, including procedures relating to their appointment, evaluation, and extent of authority. We will also describe operating procedures in each state including caseload, types of cases, and lines of communication between each of the pools and the agencies it services. In so doing, we will highlight the broad differences and similarities among the seven systems.

4. The hearing process and the role of the ALJ

To explore the impact of the pool approach on the administrative hearing, we have examined, in Chapter 5 and 6, the daily roles of the ALJ through both interviews with directors and a questionnaire survey of the ALJs themselves. We begin by profiling the central panel ALJs—their method of appointment, term of office, qualifications for office, and means of recruitment. We also inquired into means used to evaluate, promote, and remove ALJs. To examine the due process rights afforded litigants, we compared hearing procedures in our seven states. Finally, we examined the impact of the ALJs' decisions on agency decisionmaking.

The issue of ALJ independence in a central pool setting is an umbrella notion, encompassing topics ranging from whether ALJs hear more than one type of case, to whether the ALJs have any contact with agency personnel, to whether ALJs should be assigned to specific types of cases because they have specialized expertise.

In general, we define ALJ independence in terms of the status of ALJs in the system—what ALJs do on a day-to-day basis and the authority they are given to accomplish their duties. We will report our findings in these areas in an attempt to better illustrate the role of the ALJ and thus to improve understanding of the independence issue.

A note on methodology

Our research method was twofold. We interviewed by telephone the directors of central panel agencies in seven states, and conducted a mail questionnaire survey of all full-time ALJs in the same seven state central panel agencies (125).

A structured interview instrument was used throughout the telephone interviews, although directors were provided ample opportunity to discuss matters at length—and often did so. Interviews, on average, were two hours long. Our inquiries were designed to obtain an overview of organizational structure. In addition, we sought to identify factors important to the implementation of each pool as well as to the maintenance of the systems. We also obtained directors' perceptions as to the relationship between the central panel and state agencies. A fourth area of focus involved directors' perceptions of the ALJ role.

Questionnaires were mailed to 125 ALJs. Questions were generally scaled and closed-ended although the instrument requested additional comments. Eighty-seven ALJs (69.6%) returned the completed questionnaires which focused on two aspects of the ALJ's role. First, we asked questions concerning the day-to-day duties of the ALJs, including their activities during administrative proceedings. Second, we asked them their perceptions of their role, including their views on the impact of the central panel on their decisionmaking, their independence, their performance evaluation, and their relationships with the agencies. In the questionnaire's last section, we gathered information to create a demographic profile of central panel ALJs. For a breakdown of mean responses to the questionnaire, see Appendix A.

NOTES

1. Pound, *Jurisprudence* (Vol. II). St. Paul: West Publishing Co. (1959).

2. One of the earliest and most prominent calls for more due process protections came from Charles Reich. Reich, "The New Property," 73 *The Yale Law Journal* 733 (1964).

3. This continues to be a primary concern among attorneys representing litigants before administrative tribunals. *See, e.g.,* Testimony of Christopher McNaughton, Senior Vice President, Corporate Services and General Counsel, Kellogg Co., Before the House Post Office and Civil Service Committee on H.R. 6768, 96th Cong., 2d Sess., April 24, 1980.

4. Substitute House Bill No. 101, enacted April 16, 1981.

5. 60 Stat. 237 (1946), as amended by 80 Stat. 378 (1966), as amended by 81 Stat. 54 (1967). 5 U.S.C. Sections 551-59, 701-06, 1305, 3105, 3344, 6362, 7562.

2
The Central Panel within the Administrative Process

A modern study of administrative law judges is not only a study of a profession but also an examination of how the political structure combines with law to create social policy. Administrative law judges are employed by both the federal and state governments to conduct hearings in which administrative determinations are made, but the type of hearings they conduct and the use the agency makes of ALJ determinations varies from agency to agency.[1] The proceedings sometimes include highly paid legal representation—and sometimes only the ALJ and an unrepresented citizen claiming government benefits.

ALJs now resemble judges in their duties as finders of facts or as decisionmakers or both. In some agencies, the ALJ decision may be only a recommendation while the agency retains final decisionmaking power. In other agencies, the ALJ ruling is final or it becomes the final decision of the agency if there is no appeal or the agency does not review the decision on its own motion. All federal ALJs' decisions, according to the Supreme Court, become part of the case record and must be considered when final agency action is reviewed by a court.[2]

The matters considered by ALJs are of critical importance both to the individual and to society generally. Some ALJs hear requests for licensing in such areas as transportation and energy. Others participate in administrative rulemaking and enforcement proceedings. Still others adjudicate claims relating to Social Security, welfare benefits, and workers' compensation. This list is far from exhaustive; but the decisions of ALJs clearly affect the way we live today.

The Federal System

Administrative agencies were established and then flourished as a blend of governmental powers in a way that would satisfy political and economic needs. As nineteenth century America experienced the Industrial Revolution, its problems grew more technological. The New Deal created complex economic questions pertaining to the relationship between the government and citizens. Administrative agencies were devised to blend executive, legislative, and judicial powers to resolve the disputes in this new environment.

In the early part of the 1900s federal administrative agencies began to employ examiners to assist them in their decisionmaking.[3] Since these officers were employees of the agencies, their compensation and job tenure were controlled by the agency. Many agencies could ignore their hearing officers' decisions and enter de novo rulings instead.[4] And they could require the officers, as agency employees, to serve as agency prosecutors. Thus, the introduction of hearings officers was not an attempt to separate adjudication from other agency functions; it was designed to promote efficiency.[5]

In 1937, criticism of the combined legislative and judicial powers of the agencies prompted President Roosevelt to appoint a committee to study the "independent regulatory commissions."[6] The committee's report characterized the administrative process as "a headless fourth branch of government," noting that the problem centered around the combination of powers within each agency.[7] At nearly the same time, Roscoe Pound, a formidable critic of administrative justice, complained that it lacked an "effective check," and emphasized the need for judicial review.[8] Thus, while some hailed a combination of powers as the main strength of the process, others saw it as a threat to impartial justice.[9]

As a counter to this "threat," Congress in 1937 passed the Logan-Walter bill, which attempted to provide a "check" on administrative action by judicializing agency procedure and providing for judicial review. President Roosevelt vetoed the bill on the ground that the administrative process should not be encumbered by judicial formality.[10] But criticism of the administrative system did not stop.

The Attorney General's Committee on Administrative Procedure proposed in 1941 to create a separate judicial power within each agency. Unlike the vetoed action, though, the Committee focused on the use of independent hearing examiners to provide intra-agency judicial-like review.[11] The Committee report marked an emerging emphasis on formalized adjudication within the administrative system. The process was to utilize an independent examiner to provide a semblance of separation of powers within the administrative process.

The report ultimately became the basis for Section 11 of the Federal Administrative Procedure Act of 1946 (FAPA).[12] According to the Act, the hearing officer is to preside over administrative proceedings and issue opinions that must be ultimately accepted or rejected by the agency to which the ALJ is assigned. The hearing officers are given career appointments, and control over compensation has been transferred from the agencies to the Civil Service Commission (now the Office of Personnel Management).[13] The hearing officer was not granted complete statutory independence, however; the FAPA allowed the officers to be assigned to a particular agency.

Since enactment of the FAPA, the evolution toward judicialized adjudication has continued. Federal court decisions have put almost judicial responsibilities on the shoulders of the hearing examiners.[14] But the Supreme Court has also expressly recognized the federal ALJ as a judicial-like figure who is not *totally* independent. The Court has ruled that Congress intended to render hearing examiners "a special class of semi-independent subordinate hearing officers by vesting control of their compensation, promotion, and tenure in the Civil Service Commission to a greater extent than in the cases of other federal employees."[15] Yet it is clear that the Court views ALJs as being independent of agency whim. In one of its most recent statements on the matter, the Court stated:

> The process of agency adjudication is currently structured so as to assure that the hearing examiner exercises his independent judgment on the evidence before him, free from pressures by the parties or other officials within the agency.[16]

The State Administrative System

The literature dealing with the federal administrative system is voluminous, but comparatively little attention has been paid to state administrative agencies. Yet state government action has had an increasingly important impact on the rights and privileges of individuals and businesses. Each state has scores of administrative agencies attempting to regulate the quality of life, and substantially more lawyers argue before state tribunals than before federal agencies. Thus, some of the same issues of efficiency and fairness affect the state systems as they do the federal. Although the federal government partially separated its hearing examiners from agencies (using the approach set for them in the 1946 FAPA), the states have not uniformly dealt with the critical problems, but instead they have taken several distinct types of approaches.

The most common approach is the agency staff system,[17] a system in which the ALJ resembles more an agency employee than a judicial figure. Although the hearings ALJs conduct concern contested cases and are characterized as judicial in nature, the ALJ remains subject to direct agency supervision. States using this system vary as to whether the ALJ's decision is presumed correct when reviewed by the agency.[18] Jurisdictional and procedural guidelines are derived from broad administrative acts, giving agencies great latitude in deploying and evaluating their ALJs.[19] The judicial "branch" under the agency staff system is thus less separate from the legislative duties of the agency than in the federal system or under other types of approaches used by states.

Within the agency staff systems, the varying purposes of agencies lead to differing approaches to the use of administrative judges. If the agency handles a large and constant amount of litigation (such as worker's compensation or unemployment insurance), it will employ ALJs on a full-time basis to preside over contested cases. If a smaller agency has neither the funds nor demand for full-time ALJs, it will often designate staff employees as temporary ALJs when contested cases emerge. Sometimes outside attorneys-at-law will serve as temporary administrative judges.[20]

It is difficult to generalize about the hearing process under the agency staff system, for each agency has the discretion to develop its own rules of procedure.[21] We present this abbreviated view of agency staff systems to provide a common example of systems in which ALJs remain within the agency, both in terms of physical location and in terms of compensation, tenure, and evaluation.

Two states though—Maine and Missouri—have gone even further than the FAPA provisions. In these states, original jurisdiction to hear contested cases is removed from the agency and given directly to an administrative court created by the state legislature.[21] The agency becomes a party litigant and the decision of the court is final, subject only to an appeal to the state court system. The jurisdiction of existing administrative courts is generally limited to cases involving licensing, however.[22]

The Model State Administrative Procedure Act
Nearly all states have adopted legislation governing their administrative procedures, just as the federal government enacted its Administrative Procedure Act to govern the federal administrative process. The model State Administrative Procedure Act (Model Act) was adopted in 1946 by the National Conference of Commissioners on Uniform State Laws to serve as a guide to the states. It was revised in 1961 and most recently in 1981 and has been adopted (with some variations) in at least 28 states.

The 1981 Model Act, like its federal APA counterpart, contains provisions aimed at the use of ALJs. It provides optional versions requiring a person to be admitted to practice law "in this state" or "in a jurisdiction in the United States" before being eligible to serve as an ALJ.[23] It also dictates that ALJ functions are to be strictly separated from the duties of other agency employees and the state ALJ is required to render an initial order that is subject to agency review (unless such review is precluded or limited by statute or agency rule). The Model Act provides for disqualification of biased ALJs, prohibits certain types of ex parte communications, requires ALJ and agency decisions to be supported by the record, and confers general powers upon ALJs for the conduct of proceedings.

Focus on the Central Panel Approach

We place the central panel between the federal approach and that of the administrative court in terms of separating ALJs from their agencies. Under this arrangement, ALJs are not employed by the agencies for which they hear cases but by a distinct agency created solely for the purpose of their management.

The scope of jurisdiction under these systems is limited by the state's administrative procedure act. Each system is individualized in other ways as well. Use of ALJs from the centralized pool is either required by agencies delineated in the state's APA or is at the discretion of the state agencies. These ALJs are located in and managed by a separate agency which assigns them to preside over hearings when state agencies so request. As with the agency staff systems, decisions of central panel ALJs are usually recommended decisions, subject to the agencies' adoption.

The 1981 Model Act establishes a central panel. Two versions allow the states to make the use of the central panel mandatory (agencies must use central panel ALJs) or permissive (agencies may use central panel ALJs) and to allow those states with existing central panels to keep them, without modifying the circumstances under which ALJs are utilized.[24] The Model Act provides for the director of the central panel to be appointed by the governor—senate confirmation is offered as an option. The director is empowered to appoint the ALJs and to assign them to cases. An agency, according to the Model Act, may neither select nor reject any individual ALJ for any proceeding except in accordance with other provisions of the Model Act (on such matters as ALJ disqualification).[25]

The federal APA sought to "insulate the hearing and deciding function from improper pressures and controls and thus assure greater fairness and objectivity."[26] Using a different approach, the central panel system has been said to seek the same objectives. For example:

> The New Jersey system,...based upon the concept of an independent administrative judiciary, goes further toward ensuring fair, high caliber decisionmaking than the federal approach and those of other states which rely upon agency affiliated hearing examiners to act as judges in cases where their employers have a stake in the outcome.[27]

The central panel was established at the state level to balance due process concerns with administrative effectiveness while retaining ALJ independence. Proponents and opponents of the system utilize this trade-off in their arguments. For example, advocates of independent ALJs

11

insist that parties to administrative action will not see the proceedings as impartial as long as the ALJ is in any way officially associated with the agency.

> [I]t is undesirable as a matter of policy for an ALJ to be used in a staff capacity, in the climate and relationship of staff assistants to their boards or commissioners. Any such role is bound to have an eroding effect upon the ALJ's independence and upon his own attitude and state of mind. It is also bound, insidiously, to have a damaging impact upon the attitude which the agency, the staff, and the parties will have toward the ALJ. The parties' confidence in the total independence and objectivity of the ALJ might be somewhat shaken or diminished if they felt that his knowledge and views as to agency policy and positions were not obtained solely from a study of the agency's published opinions but were molded and influenced by private informal discussions with agency members.[28]

As the administrative judge moved away from those agency connections and as the process moved toward judicialization, with its focus on providing justice in a new forum, it has collided with an emerging emphasis on expedient resolution of conflicts. Thus, those within the administrative process concerned with providing due process protections for litigants and maintaining ALJ independence must balance these values against new demands for productivity in the administrative system.

The seven states that have initiated a new approach to administrative adjudication place ALJs in an independent agency—a central panel or pool. This office, which assigns ALJs to state agencies when they request them to conduct administrative hearings, aims to promote more objective and efficient adjudication by separating ALJs from the agencies they serve. Thus, ALJs can serve more than one agency without being employed by any one of them. The idea is not without critics, of course; some see the central panel as a further usurping of the powers of agencies that used to directly employ ALJs—a sort of "creeping judicialization" that threatens the effectiveness of the administrative process.[29]

Unfortunately, it is easier to find reports of the debate than to find studies on the central panel system. No one has explored this new system very extensively to see what its common features are and what participants think of it. That is the broad purpose of the study on which we report here.

Advantages of the Central Panel
Throughout its existence, administrative adjudication has been faced with a trade-off between providing a fair proceeding for the litigants and providing justice expediently. One result of the trade-off has been an ongoing tension between agency policymakers and hearing officers who must apply those policies to everyday occurrences. The central pool

12

system attempts to alleviate the tension by separating the hearing officers from the agency officials and thereby better define the role of each.

In these days of government budget cutting, administrative agencies are hard pressed to decide how much due process is enough—how much they can *afford* to give litigants. From a jurisprudential point of view, the central panel approach seeks to provide due process of law through a separation of legislative and judicial powers. But it offers a variety of other advantages, too, according to its advocates:[30]

- Its proponents claim that by more efficiently allocating hearing examiners the system is less expensive than assigning ALJs permanently to one agency. Larger agencies will not have to keep all the ALJs they need to handle cases during peak periods. Smaller agencies will always have ALJs available to them without having to pay larger sums to hire practicing lawyers, for example, to serve as temporary ALJs.
- If ALJs are not permanently attached to an agency, proponents say, they may feel compelled to write longer, more reasoned justifications for their decisions.[31]
- Central panel ALJs can hear a variety of cases so that they will always be approaching a problem from a fresh perspective.[32]
- A central pool allows one administrative staff to handle the bookkeeping related to the employment of ALJs. And locating ALJs in one office allows administrative cost-cutting innovations to be implemented.[33]

Disadvantages of the Central Panel
The first of two articulated disadvantages is that the central panel office will become a "super agency"—that it will develop collective policies and procedures that usurp the powers of the administrative agencies. One critic of central panels insists that:

> Where examiners are employed within the agency, there is much less tendency for the examiner to encroach upon policymaking.[34]

Opponents of the central pool claim the idea is another step toward judicialization and is, therefore, another step toward reducing the power of agency officials. However, some proponents of the approach see this as a benefit. The conflict stems from the trade-off between due process and administrative effectiveness that administrators claim they need to make and implement policies. Judicialization is, in this view, an unnecessary shackling of that discretion. The further the ALJs are from the agencies, the greater the shackling of the administrators. Yet it is this administrative discretion that some proponents wish to confine by means of the central panel notion.

The second alleged disadvantage is related to organizational structure. Opponents think that placing all decisions relating to ALJs' employment in the hands of just one agency (and in the hands of one director) risks creating the appearance of (or actually create) a different kind of bias. Central panel directors—often political appointees—are responsible for decisions relating to hiring, promoting, evaluation and setting salary of ALJs. Opponents view this arrangement as potentially creating a non-objective environment for hearings.

Conclusion

We have attempted in this chapter to place the central panel approach in perspective. Like the federal system and the administrative court concept, the centralized pool seeks to separate ALJs from the agencies they serve. Unlike its counterparts, the central panel allows its ALJs to serve more than one agency without being employed by any one of them. The result, say proponents, is a more objective and efficient system of administrative justice. Opponents, however, see this movement as a sort of "creeping judicialization" that threatens the effectiveness of the administrative process. These arguments have become increasingly important as more attempts are made to change the regulatory system.

Discussion of the administrative system has, in recent years, been pervaded by such terms as "independence," "discretion," "evaluation," and "expertise." Legislation designed to affect the selection, evaluation, and tenure of federal ALJs has been introduced but not enacted.[35] But in the process, the bills have led some to examine the state procedures for possible new role models. As a result, new attention has been paid to the central panel approach as a possible model for the federal system. In September, 1980, Senator Howell Heflin (D-Alabama) chaired hearings on the administrative law judge system during which he explored the possibility of a central panel system for the federal administrative agencies and the problems that would accompany it.[36]

What has emerged from these hearings and other debates on the use of ALJs is that there is little information on state administrative adjudication. The central panel has taken its place within the spectrum of the administrative system, but critical questions relating to its effectiveness and feasibility remain unanswered. Part of this problem lies in the newness of these operations, yet part can be linked to an emphasis on debating the policy questions surrounding the usage of ALJs without exploring what administrative judges do on a day-to-day basis. The place of the central panel within the administrative process can be defined only after there is a thorough understanding of the duties and responsibilities of state ALJs and agency officials alike. Without such an understanding, the advantages and disadvantages of the central panel will remain speculative.

NOTES

1. There were 1,166 federal ALJs as of June, 1981, while over 3,000 hearing officers preside over state administrative adjudication.

2. Universal Camera Corp. v. NLRB, 340 U.S. 474 (1951). This concept is generally accepted in state administrative law as well. *See, e.g.,* cases cited in note 18, *infra.*

3. For an overview, *see* Nathanson, "Social Science, Administrative Law, and the Information Act of 1966," 21 *Social Problems* 21 (1973), or Pops, "The Judicialization of Federal Administrative Law Judges: Implications for Policymaking," 81 *West Virginia L. Rev.* 169 (1979).

4. *See* F. Davis, "Judicialization of Administrative Law: The Trial-Type Hearing and the Changing Status of the Hearing Officer," 1977 *Duke L. J.* 389 (1977).

5. *Id.*

6. Nathanson, *supra* note 3, at 22.

7. *Id.*

8. Pound, *Jurisprudence* (Vol. II). (St. Paul: West Publishing Company, 1959).

9. Among those seeing this main strength was Dean James Landis, who in his 1938 lectures at the Yale Law School stated that the combination of powers was well suited to the "special missions" of administrative agencies. *See* Nathanson, *supra* note 3, at 22.

10. "Logan-Walter Bill Fails," 27 *A.B.A.J.* 52 (January 1941).

11. *Attorney General's Committee on Administrative Procedure, Administrative Procedure in Government Agencies,* S. Doc. No. 8, 77th Cong., 1st Sess. 47 (1941).

12. *See* Chapter 1, note 5, *supra.*

13. 5 U.S.C. Sec. 5362 and Sec. 7521.

14. One example was the 1947 case of NLRB v. Donnelly Garment Co., 330 U.S. 319 (1947). There Justice Frankfurter analogized hearing examiners to judges, saying: "… [C] ertainly it is not the rule of judicial administration that a judge is disqualified from sitting in a retrial because he was reversed on earlier rulings. We find no warrant for imposing upon administrative agencies a stiffer rule whereby examiners would be disentitled to sit because they rule strongly against a party in the first hearing." 330 U.S. at 23.

15. 345 U.S. 128, 130-31 (1953). For an in-depth discussion of the role of the federal ALJ, *see* Rosenblum, "The Administrative Law Judge in the Administrative Process: Interrelations of Case Law with Statutory and Pragmatic Factors in Determining ALJ Roles," printed in Subcomm. on Social Security of the House Comm. on Ways and Means, 94th Cong., 1st Sess., *Recent Studies Relevant to the Disability Hearings and Appeals Crisis 171* (Comm. Print, December 20, 1975).

16. Butz v. Economou, 438 U.S. 478, 513 (1978).

17. For an overview, *see* Cooper, *State Administrative Law* Vol. 1 (New York: Bobbs-Merrill, 1965).

18. *See, e.g.,* the following cases for discussion of this issue: Kimball v. Hawkins, 364 So. 2d 463 (Fla. 1978); Real Estate Comm'n v. Horne, 233 S.E. 2d 16 (Ga. App. 1977): Burton v. Illinois Civil Serv. Comm'n, 373 N.E. 2d 765 (Ill. App. 1978); St. Vincent's Hospital v. Finley, 380 A. 2d 1152 (N.J Super. 1977); Voight v. Washington Island Ferry Line, Inc., 255 N.W. 2d 545 (Wis. 1977). *See generally* Levinson, "The central panel system: a framework that separates ALJs from administrative agencies," 65 *Judicature* 236, 242-43 (1981).

19. Cooper, *supra* note 17.

20. *Id.*

21. *Id.*

22. *See* Levinson, *supra* note 18, at 242-43.

23. Article IV of the 1981 Model Act contains provisions pertaining to the presiding officer specifically and adjudication generally. For a discussion of the Model Act, *see* Levinson, *supra* note 18.

24. *Id.*

25. *Id.*

26. Macy, "The APA and the Hearing Examiner: Product of a Viable Political Society," 27 *Fed. Bar J.* 351 (1967).

27. Kestin, "Reform of the Administrative Process," 92 *New Jersey Lawyer* 35 (1980).

28. Zwerdling, "Reflections on the Role of an Administrative Judge," 25 *Admin. L. Rev.* 9 (1973).

29. This term was used by Professor Antonin Scalia of the University of Chicago Law School during the ABA Conference on the Role of the Judge in the 1980s. Washington, D.C., June 1980.

30. For a further discussion of advantages and disadvantages of the central panel, *see* Lubbers, "A unified corps of ALJs: a proposal to test the idea at the federal level," 65 *Judicature* 266 (1981), citing Digest of Report of Committee on Independent Corps of ALJ (Appendix to *Report of the Comittee on the Study of the Utilization of Administrative Law Judges*—"La Macchia Commission Report," U.S. Civil Service Comm'n, 1974).

31. *Hearings on Administrative Law Judge System Before the Subcommittee for Consumers of the Senate Committee on Commerce, Science, and Transportation*, 96th Cong., 2d Sess. 28 (September 4-5, 1980) (Testimony of Judge William Fauver).

32. Pfeiffer, "Hearing Cases Before Several Agencies—Odyssey of an Administrative Law Judge," 27 *Admin. L. Rev.* 217 (1975); and Scalia, "The Hearing Examiner Loan Program," 1971 *Duke L.J.* 319 (1971).

33. Lubbers, *supra* note 30, at 274.

34. Lakusta, "Operations in an Agency not Subject to the APA: Public Utilities Commission," 44 *Cal. L. Rev.* 218 (1956).

35. Legislation dealing specifically with the ALJ was pending as Senate bill 262 and as House bill 6768. Under the bills, the Administrative Conference of the U.S. would become responsible for selecting ALJs. Furthermore, the chairman of the Administrative Conference would establish performance and qualification review boards, a majority of whose members would be administative law judges. The evaluation boards would "conduct evaluations" and "make recommendations" to the chairman "relating to the performance and qualification of administrative law judges."

These evaluations would be required at the end of the term of office also established by the legislation—every seven years (H.R. 6768) or ten years (S. 262). Unless an ALJ was approved, he or she could not be reappointed. In addition, the ALJs would be subject under the legislation to performance evaluation during the term of office. The chairman of the Administrative Conference could, at any time, file a complaint with the Merit Systems Protection Board. The Board could then conduct a separate hearing and if the ALJ's performance was found unacceptable, could order reduction in grade or removal from office. For further discussion, *see* "Congress hears proposals for 'performance reviews' of ALJs," 63 *Judicature*, 144 (1979).

Neither bill became law but they were symptomatic of vigorous requests by some that the ALJ-type "hidden" judiciary be made more accountable.

36. *Hearings on Administrative Law Judge System Before the Subcommittee on Commerce, Science, and Transportation*, 96th Cong., 2d Sess. 28 (September 4-5, 1980).

3
The Process of Implementation

In each of the seven states we studied, the central panel system was implemented within an existing structure of administrative adjudication. The central panel systems were designed to make administrative adjudication appear to be more objective as well as to provide services more effectively. But the debate over the results is only part of the controversy; the act of implementing these systems also spurred conflicts that at times threatened the existence of these panels. These were planned changes which had and continue to have an impact on the interests, values, and established practices of ALJs and agency personnel. It is thus not surprising that efforts to implant a central panel have met resistance.[1]

The change process consists of two general components. First, each of the panels was created through the actions of state legislatures, which established the broad duties and limits of the central panel in each state. Thus, our look at the implementation process begins with legislative battles that initially shaped the panels. Our search into these legislative actions was generally limited to discussions with current directors. While this method is far from exhaustive, many of these directors were involved with shaping the enabling legislation and were part of the resulting legislative debates. We identify some of the proponents and opponents— and why they took their positions. We also focus on how the debates surrounding implementation shaped the resulting structure of central pools.

A second aspect of the change process has to do with potential problems during the time the change took place. A substantial structural change modifies the duties and authority of many people. It galvanizes resistance. We asked the directors how ALJs reacted as they became part of a pool, and, from the other perspective, asked how agency officials reacted to the change.

A third aspect of implementation is the budgeting process. We examined this aspect of implementation because while devising a reform measure is one thing, it is quite another to implement it. Sometimes what appears to be less important to the process becomes the key factor.

Reasons for the pool system are often couched in terms of independence and appearance of justice, but financial considerations have proven to be an important factor in passing the enabling legislation and in shaping the structure once approval is given by the legislature. Thus, we identify methods in which the central panel approach changed the way states pay for hearings. We asked the directors whether the type of funding affected agency acceptance of the central panel approach and in what ways it continues to affect central panel/agency relationships.

Views of Implementation

The oldest central panel in existence can be found in California. Begun in the 1940s, the debates surrounding it occurred at about the same time arguments were being made in relation to the federal Administrative Procedure Act.[2] The California system ultimately became a model for panels established much later.

As with the federal APA, the impetus for centralized ALJs in California occurred during the 1930s. The Supreme Court of California issued a 1936 opinion stating that judicial review of administrative action was no longer to be available through a writ of certiorari thereby restricting the ability of the California courts to review administrative action.[3] The state Bar of California, in response, established study committees to make recommendations to the legislature on approaches to administrative reform. In 1938, the Bar issued a report seeking separation of the prosecuting and adjudication functions in state agencies, and an adequate procedure for judicial review of administrative decisions.[4]

The Judicial Council of California was directed by the legislature in 1941 to undertake studies of judicial review of administrative decisions and the need for changes in the procedures of regulatory agencies. The proposals were limited to the field of licensing, for the Council felt it was the area of administrative practice most in need of change.[5]

The studies produced three proposals that were ultimately embodied in the California APA of 1946. First, a new Department of Administrative Procedure was to devote "continuous and expert" attention to the operation and procedure of the state's administrative agencies. The Department was also to furnish home base for a central panel of ALJs. A second proposal called for the formation of an Administrative Procedure Act and a third recommended that the California Code of Civil Procedure be amended to allow judicial review of administrative decisions by a writ of mandamus. This last suggestion was a legislative override of the 1936 California Supreme Court decision which had rejected judicial review of this type.[6]

These proposals eventually became law, but the enabling statutes covered adjudication only for the licensing agencies. The thrust of these reforms provided a new emphasis on the conduct of hearings. All hearings were to provide due process of law and were to be conducted in an orderly manner. Another important objective was to separate prosecuting and adjudicating functions within agencies.

Initially, the pool was made voluntary for licensing agencies wishing to use its services. Ultimately, the California APA was amended to make the pool mandatory for licensing agencies delineated in the Act.[7] However, the central pool still does not cover other agencies.

Following the enactment of a central panel system in California, other states began to enact state Administrative Procedure Acts. Tennessee and Massachusetts each established a centralized system in 1974. The Tennessee system was created when the 1974 Tennessee Administrative Procedure Act was enacted.[8] However, the central panel agency—the Administrative Procedures Division (APD)—was not established as a central panel. It was created to hold hearings for the small boards and commissions under Public Health and Insurance. Later the Tennessee APA was amended to state that agencies which were not authorized to have their own hearing officers were required to use the APD and other agencies could elect to use central panel hearing officers. As more agencies began to use the office, the system evolved into a central panel.[9]

Even though the APD was initially not intended to be a central panel, its creation represented change. During the legislative battles, the current director of the APD reports a common theme—that the opposition was from agencies that were "resistant to change." "Each agency has its own way of doing things and they were not happy with this system whereby the agency itself lost a considerable amount of power," he said.[10]

A similar story of resistance to implementation can be found in the Massachusetts Division of Hearing Officers (DHO). This system, like that in Tennessee, was not created as a central panel and now, in addition to providing ALJs to agencies that are required by statute to use DHO ALJs, allows agencies to utilize central panel ALJs on a voluntary basis. The DHO was created in 1974 to hear appeals from the State Rate Setting Commission. One year later the DHO became a wider reaching central panel when its enabling statute was amended to allow it to hear cases of other agencies at their request.[11]

Central panels are often part of sweeping reforms in state administrative procedure. Still another example is the Florida Division of Administrative Hearings (DAH), which began operations in November of 1974. It came about as part of a broad administrative reform effort during which Florida substituted a new administrative procedure act. The thrust of the change involved rulemaking as opposed to hearings. At the heart of the creation of the central panel was great concern over agencies' use of rulemaking to accomplish what they could not do by statute. The appearance of justice was a critical factor in convincing the legislature to include a pool system within the Florida APA.[12]

Fiscal matters were of prime importance to the Colorado central pool, which was initiated in the autumn of 1976. Unlike Tennessee and Massachusetts, nearly all Colorado agencies were required to use the hearing officers within the Division of Hearing Officers (DHO). The catalyst for the creation of the panel reportedly was the Attorney General's office, which wished to promote decisionmaking independence and cost-cutting. Largely because proponents made arguments "selling" the panel on its fiscal impact, "the legislation seemed to slip through without anybody noticing," said one respondent.[13]

Agency and ALJ Response

The interplay of changing ALJ roles and politics spawned a competition among special interests in all seven systems. Some agency officials saw in the legislative debates an attempt to replace their administrative authority with the inflexible rule of law. As one writer has noted,

> To the administrator, as we have shown before, issues are defined as social problems that call for action with a view to the accomplishment of some determinate result. The emphasis on expertise and discretion in the implementation of policy is an outcome of this orientation toward concrete action. To the adjudicator, on the contrary, issues are structured as competing moral claims, involving an appeal to principle, and which call for a determination of authoritativeness.[14]

Proponents of the legislation saw separating ALJs from agencies as a way to improve the administration of justice as well as to enhance the job status of ALJs. Agency personnel saw the same legislation as an attempt both to reduce the effectiveness of the process and to restrict the agencies' ability to take action toward solving social problems. Directors of central panels in Massachusetts and Minnesota as well as in Florida report that one impetus for creating the pools was displeasure among some legislatures with agency "rulemaking by fiat."[15] Agencies had been adopting rules without public input, which prompted a perceived need to add a sort of "check" on agency discretion.

Directors who were familiar with the legislative debates reported fierce opposition by the agencies during both the debates and the changeover period. This reaction was characterized as "a large amount of animosity" (Florida) and "initial agency resistance" (Tennessee).[16] In Massachusetts the symptoms of the reaction appeared in the ways agency personnel reacted to the ALJs:

At first, the rate setting commissioners still seemed to think that the hearing officers were still subordinate to their wishes.[17]

The directors in Tennessee reported that agencies there were "very angry and upset. They traditionally used their hearing officers for a number of functions besides hearing cases. They didn't want to lose the hearing officers from those functions."[18]

On the other hand, the ALJs, according to the directors, were generally pleased to become part of a central pool. The main attractions included an increased variety of cases, independence, and somewhat higher pay than they would have received as non-central panel ALJs. ALJs' reaction to the independence question bore out the views of the directors. More than half of those questioned commented on the value of being separate from the agency.[19] However, some of the ALJs transferred into the central pools had been attached to other agencies, and thus had been hearing one type of case for long periods of time. The change to hearing a variety of cases created for some ALJs, as well as agency officials, a substantial modification of work behavior that sometimes resulted in friction among the systems' principal actors.

A related problem also involved the inherent structure of the pool system. At the outset, ALJs who had been assigned to agencies were transferred into pool systems and assigned to hear cases for their former agencies as independent presiding officers. Sometimes disputes with former agencies spilled into the role of the central pool ALJ. One example can be found in the changeover period in Minnesota: For two years animosity between hearing officers and their former agencies appeared in what one observer described as "cheap shots" being taken by ALJs—pointed comments directed against agency officials within ALJ decisions.[20]

The Role of the Bar

Agency personnel and ALJs were not the only interested parties in the legislative action leading to the pool systems. The state bar associations were important factors in many of the debates. For example, the Minnesota Bar Association was a primary force behind the formulation of the Minnesota pool, which began operations in 1976. The current Minnesota director worked with the Bar for three years prior to the creation of the Office of Administrative Hearings (OAH), the Minnesota central panel agency. The Bar's rationale for so vigorously pursuing the central panel was to reduce delay and to enhance the appearance of justice.[21]

But its role was consistent with previous actions of bar associations in general as representatives of the legal community. They have been in the forefront of many reform efforts aimed at increased judicialization of federal administrative efforts. The bar vigorously supported federal legislation during the 1930s which, had it been enacted, would have established intra-agency, judicial-like review mechanisms. The bar also promoted the 1946 Administrative Procedure Act, which created a more independent corp of federal ALJs, and in 1972 the bar was a motivating force behind changing the title of hearing examiner to administrative law judge.[22]

Despite the efforts of the Bar in Minnesota, however, the panel was created as part of political compromise. Agencies in each of the seven states opposed the approach but apparently did not have the political clout to obstruct the legislation. The result was different when organized labor actively opposed the panel system in Minnesota. The original legislation provided that the Office of Administrative Hearings (the central panel) would service the areas of unemployment compensation, workers' compensation, and the Bureau of Mediation Services, among other areas. As a result, organized labor lobbied against the bill, preventing its passage. The authors of the bill then exempted these agencies and the bill was quickly enacted. Recently, though, the Minnesota central panel was given jurisdiction over the area of workers' compensation.[23]

The New Jersey State Bar Association was an important force in creating that state's Office of Administrative Law (OAL) in 1979, which was the result of a movement for the central panel that reportedly spanned a period of 30 years. The New Jersey director reports that the modern stimulus occurred when a former deputy attorney general and active member of the administrative law section of the state Bar became counsel to the governor.[24] The governor, in turn, became an active supporter of the central panel concept and helped quell the related dissatisfaction among agency officials.

When the bill passed, it contained a statement of legislative purpose not altogether different from its counterparts in the other six states:

> The purpose of this legislation is to improve the quality of justice with respect to administrative hearings. In many agencies, hearing officers served on a part-time basis. They are either self-employed persons who are paid per diem to hold hearings for state agencies or they are state employees who also perform other duties for their agency in addition to holding hearings. In both instances, a hearing officer frequently presides over cases in which his own employee is an interested party. In some agencies, the backlog of cases is extensive and some administrative hearings have been cited as examples of faulty procedure.
>
> The legislative goal embodied in this bill is to create a central independent agency staffed by professionals with the sole function of conducting administrative hearings. This will tend to eliminate conflict of interests...promote due process, expedite the just conclusion of contested cases and generally improve the quality of administrative justice.[25]

Budgetary Considerations

Implementing a central panel transfers some degree of financial control from the agency to the panel. No longer do the agencies have exclusive administrative and financial control of the hearing process, and as a result, the system is a potential source of conflict. These concerns have become evident both during the changeover period as well as during legislative debates. What is most striking is the lack of hard data on budgetary issues. State legislatures consider the cost effectiveness of these systems as much as any other issue, yet most claims are based on gross bottom line figures or on "gut reaction."

We explored the ways in which central pools are funded and the possibility that funding techniques affect the degree to which agencies accept and generally utilize the panel notion. We report the theories relayed to us by directors and other sources with the caveat that none has been conclusively established.

A cost effectiveness study was begun by a member of the Minnesota legislature, but it was not completed because agencies reportedly refused to provide data on hearing costs prior to the OAH.[26] This raises a key factor in examining the issue of budget. The directors say the system is cost effective but their views are often subjective, since conclusive cost figures are not available.

The director of the New Jersey system reports his system is cost effective "as a matter of absolute certainty," but the agencies are not willing to acknowledge the accuracy of the statement. He has developed figures showing that before the Office of Administrative Law was established the agencies were spending $5.5 million on direct hearing costs while under the OAL the budget was $4.0 million.[27] Similarly, the director in Minnesota points to a before/after reduction in bottom line expenditures. At the time the Minnesota panel was established, the Public Service Commission had a $400,000 1975 annual budget to pay its in-house hearing examiners and court reporters. During the first year of the Office of Administrative Hearings, the Commission's hearing costs were reduced to $313,330 and its projected fiscal 1981 budget is still lower—$275,000.[28]

However, these bottom line comparisons do not take into account changes in patterns of ALJ usage during the time considered. Reasons for the declining expenditures (other than the use of the central panel) have not been thoroughly explored.

Two Methods of Funding

Existing operations are funded in one of two ways. One approach is known as general funding. The state legislature appropriates a set amount of money which it transfers to the central panel agency to use as an operating budget. The other approach is the revolving fund, in which the central panel bills agencies for the use of its hearing services on an hourly basis (See Table 3-1). Under revolving funding, the agencies are appropriated funds by the state legislature. Opinion was split among the directors we interviewed as to which system is preferable but all agreed the pool notion is more cost efficient than assigning ALJs permanently to one agency.

The Hearing Examiners' Section of the Minnesota Office of Administrative Hearings (OAH) operates on a fully revolving fund. Agencies are billed at the fiscal 1981 rate of $40 per hour but this figure is adjusted yearly. Generally, the OAH derives this hourly rate by providing agencies with figures on their hearing expenditures over the two preceding years. The agencies then project their needs in terms of hearing examiner hours. The OAH compares these figures with the amount it must charge per hour to meet its fixed costs and expenses and the agencies are appropriated the billing rate times the number of hours projected.[29] The portion of the OAH providing administrative judges for workers' compensation proceedings is funded through the state's general fund, however.

Colorado's system operates in a way similar to that of Minnesota, but the panels in Massachusetts, Florida, and Tennessee function within a budget appropriated to them by the legislature. Using past experience and estimates supplied by the agencies, the directors propose a budget which must then be appropriated by the state.[30]

The third approach is a hybrid. Current bills in New Jersey are paid by general funds appropriated to the central panel agency. However, agencies are also given a budget for hearing services, and are then billed by the central panel on a fixed rate basis.[31]

How a pool is funded is both a question of economic efficiency and a political issue. It is not clear whether one approach is more cost efficient than the other, but it has been theorized that type of funding will affect agency use of ALJ services. The director in Florida, for example, spoke in

Table 3-1
Central Panel Systems: Methods of Funding

California	Revolving Fund
Colorado	Revolving Fund
Florida	General Revenue
Massachusetts	General Revenue
Minnesota	Revolving Fund (Hearing Examiners' Section)
	General Fund (Workers' Compensation Section)
New Jersey	Revolving Fund/General Revenue
Tennessee	General Revenue

opposition to the revolving fund system. The Florida APA originally provided for a revolving fund, but the legislature funded the first year of operation through a general trust fund. The Department of Administrative Hearings successfully sought an elimination of the revolving fund notion on the ground that billing the agencies will encourage them to avoid hearings by settling more often. Another hypothesis is that agencies will request fewer hearings near the end of the fiscal year when the budget line-item for hearings grows thin.[32] But other opponents of the revolving fund argue that the method will produce the opposite result. The concern is that once an agency has a budget for hearings, it will send cases it considers frivolous or politically sensitive to the central panel for resolution.

No Final Answer

No evidence conclusively points to either of these hypotheses. In fact, one may imagine that the latter result (overuse) can occur under a general revenue system in which an agency does not pay on a case-by-case basis. The general acceptance of the central panel notions by the agencies may be as important if not more important than the type of funding. But budgetary considerations raise a practical problem that is influenced by funding method. What occurs if the agency (under a revolving system) or the central panel (under a general revenue system) runs out of money? The New Jersey director voiced this concern when discussing the revolving system.

> The agencies give the OAL (Office of Administrative Law) cases with impunity and then scream when the OAL bills them. They cry poor— which is often a legitimate cry—but the money must come from somewhere.[33]

The potential problem has been addressed in Minnesota. There, if an agency depletes its budget for hearings, it petitions the Legislative Advisory Commission. This body meets quarterly and is composed of members of the legislature. It may elect to provide additonal funds to agencies from a state contingency fund. An alternative resolution of funding shortages is a supplemental appropriations bill.

One of the reasons that the impact of funding methods is not clearly understood is the newness of these systems and an inadequate system of data collection. Under central panel systems, however, either the agencies or the central panel directors need to make accurate forecasts of requirements for hearings so that realistic budget appropriations can be made.

NOTES

1. This was the situation described by many of the directors of central panel systems to whom we spoke. For a further discussion of the impact of planned change, *see* Grau, "The

Limits of Planned Change in the Courts," 6/1 *The Justice System Journal* 84 (1981).

2. Clarkson, "The History of the California Administrative Procedure Act," 15 *The Hastings L. J.* 237 (1964).

3. *Id.*

4. *Id.*

5. *Id.*

6. *Id.* Standard Oil Co. v. Board of Equalization, 59 P.2d 119 (Cal. 1936).

7. For a further discussion of the California system, *see* Abrams, "Administrative Law Judge Systems: The California View," 29 *Admin. L. Rev.* 487 (1977).

8. Tenn. Code Ann. Sections 4-5-101—4-5-121.

9. Interview with director of Tennessee central panel, September 1980.

10. *Id.*

11. Interview with director of Massachusetts central panel, September 1980.

12. Interview with director of Florida central panel, September 1980.

13. Interview with director of Colorado central panel, September 1980.

14. Nonet, *Administrative Justice, Advocacy and Change in a Government Agency*. New York: Russell Sage Foundation (1969).

15. Interviews with directors, September-October 1980.

16. *Id.*

17. Interview with director of Massachusetts central panel, September 1980.

18. Interview, September 1980.

19. The questionnaire allowed open-ended responses.

20. The Chief Hearing Examiner in Minnesota reports that this problem has been resolved.

21. Interview with Chief Hearing Examiner in Minnesota, September 1980.

22. *See* "Logan-Walter Bill Fails," 27 *A.B.A.J.* 52 (January 1941) and F. Davis, "Judicialization of Administrative Law: The Trial Type Hearing and the Changing Status of the Hearing Officer," 1977 *Duke L.J.* 389 (1977).

23. Interview with Chief Hearing Examiner in Minnesota, September 1980. The Office is now comprised of both a Hearing Examiners' Section and a Workers' Compensation Section.

24. Interview with director of New Jersey central panel, September 1980.

25. N.J. Stat. Ann. Section 52:14F-1.

26. Interview with Chief Hearing Examiner in Minnesota, September 1980.

27. Kestin, "Reform of the Administrative Process," 92 *New Jersey Lawyer* 35 (1980).

28. Harves, "Making administrative proceedings more efficient and effective: how the ALJ central panel system works in Minnesota," 65 *Judicature* 257 (1981).

29. *Id.*

30. Interviews with directors, September-October 1980.

31. Interview with director of New Jersey central panel, September 1980.

32. Riccio, "Due Process in Quasi-Judicial Administrative Hearings: Confining the Examiner to One Hat," 2 *Seaton Hall L.J.* 398 (1971).

33. Interview, September 1980.

4
The Structure of Central Panels

If the seven operating central panel systems share the notion of separating ALJs from agencies, they are nevertheless different in terms of daily operating procedures. The panels can be distinguished, for example, on the basis of jurisdiction—which agencies must utilize the services provided by the central panel ALJs—and the varying powers they give the central panel director. In this chapter, we focus on the similarities and differences in the ways central panel agencies are structured. Then, in the next chapter, we examine the role of the ALJs within these structures.

Jurisdiction

The scope of central panel operations is dictated by the state legislatures through the state administrative procedure acts (See Table 4-1). Over a period of time, several means of using central panel ALJs have emerged. In general, jurisdiction can be considered either mandatory (agencies listed in the state APA must use central panel ALJs) or voluntary (agencies may use the central panel services).

The first panel, begun in California in 1946, originally was granted a "hybrid" jurisdiction.[1] The agencies could either use their own hearing officers or those in the centralized pool. Agencies who had their own hearing officers often continued to use them, thereby limiting the effect of centralized hearing officers on the system.[2] The approach was intended to create an administrative judge that was more independent of the agencies, but the jurisdiction that was provided served to circumvent that objective.

> Under the system, central panel hearing officers were at an automatic disadvantage in the competitive situation into which they were thrust, a fact that affected morale and may have subtly influenced decisions.[3]

In 1961, the California APA was amended to require all agencies to which the APA was applicable to use only central panel hearing officers. Today, over 70 agencies are required to use these administrative judges.[4]

Table 4-1
Summary of Key Features of Central Panel Systems

State	Panel began operations	Official title of central panel	Statutory mandate
California	1945	Office of Administrative Hearings	Cal. Gov't Code §§11370.2, 11502
Colorado	1976	Division of Hearing Officers	Colo. Rev. Stat. §24-30-1001
Florida	1974	Division of Administrative Hearings	Fla. Stat. Ann. §120.65
Massachusetts	Began: 1974 Expanded: 1975	Division of Hearing Officers	Mass. Ann. Laws Ch. 7 §4H
Minnesota	1976	Office of Administrative Hearings	Minn. Stat. Ann. §15.052
New Jersey	1979	Office of Administrative Law	N.J. Stat. Ann. §52:14F-1, §52:14B-1
Tennessee	1974	Administrative Procedures Division	Tenn. Code Ann. §§4-5-321

Table 4-2
Jurisdiction of Seven Central Panel Systems

Blanket Administrative Procedure Act Coverage—All agencies utilize central panel services (Exceptions noted)	Specifically Enumerated Agencies Must Use Central Panel Services (Specific agencies noted)	Use of Central Panel Services Voluntary (Exceptions noted)
Colorado (Col. Rev. Stat. §24-30-1003—Public Utility Comm'n)	**California** (Cal. Gov't Code §11501) See Note 3	**Massachusetts** (State Rate Setting Comm'n; Civil Service Comm'n; State Contrib. Retirement Appeal Bd.)
Florida (Fla. Stat. Ann. §120.57) See Note 1		**Tennessee** (Bds. under Dept. of Insurance and Dept. of Public Health; any agency without statutory authority to use its own ALJs.)
Minnesota (Minn. Stat. Ann. §15.041 (Subd. 3)) See Note 2		
New Jersey (N.J. Stat. Ann. §52:14F-8—State Board of Parole; Public Employees Relations Comm'n; Division of Workers' Comp.; Division of Tax Appeals)		

Note 1. Florida Statutes Annotated §120.57 (in relevant part)
The provisions of this section shall apply in all proceedings in which the substantial interests of a party are determined by an agency. Unless waived by all parties, subsection (1) shall apply whenever the proceeding involves a disputed issue of material fact....
(1) Formal proceedings.—
(a) A hearing officer assigned by the division shall conduct all hearings under this subsection, except for:
1. Hearings before agency heads or a member thereof other than an agency head or a member of an agency head within the Department of Professional and Occupational Regulation;
2. Hearings before the Unemployment Appeals Commission in unemployment compensation appeals, unemployment compensation appeals referees, special deputies pursuant to §443.15;
3. Hearings regarding drivers' licensing pursuant to chapter 322;
4. Hearings conducted within the Department of Health and Rehabilitative Services in the execution of those social and economic programs administered by the former Division of Family Services of said department prior to the reorganization effected by chapter 75-48, Laws of Florida;

5. Hearings in which the division is a party, in which case an attorney assigned by the Administration Commission shall be the hearing officer;

6. Hearings which involve student disciplinary suspensions or expulsions and which are conducted by educational units;

7. Hearings of the Public Employees Relations Commission[1] in which a determination is made of the appropriateness of the bargaining unit, as provided in §447.307; and

8. Hearings held by the Department of Agriculture and Consumer Services pursuant to chapter 601.

Note 2. Exempt from contested case provisions: Minnesota Municipal Board, Corrections Board, Unemployment Insurance Program in Department of Economic Security, Director of Mediation Services, Worker's Compensation Divison of Department of Labor & Industry (except for contested workers' compensation hearings), Worker's Compensation Court of Appeals, Board of Pardons, Public Employee's Relations Board, State Board of Investments, and certain welfare appeals.

Note 3. California Government Code §11501 (in relevant part)

(b) **The enumerated agencies** referred to in Section 11500 are:

Accountancy, State Board of

Aging, State Department of

Air Resources Board, State

Alcohol and Drug Abuse, State Department of

Alcoholic Beverage Control, Department of

Architectural Examiners, California State Board of

Attorney General

Automotive Repair, Bureau of

Barbers Examiners, State Board of

Behavioral Science Examiners, Board of

Cancer Advisory Council

Cemetary Board

Chiropractic Examiners, Board of

Collection and Investigative Services, Bureau of

Community Colleges, Board of Governors of the California

Conservation, Department of

Consumer Affairs, Director of

Contractors, Registrar of

Corporations, Commissioner of

Cosmetology, State Board of

Dental Examiners of California, Board of

Developmental Services, State Department of

Education, State Board of

Employment Agencies, Bureau of

Engineers, State Board of Registration for Professional

Fabric Care, State Board of

Fair Employment and Housing Commission

Fair Political Practices Commission

Fire Marshall, State

Fire Services, State Board of

Fish and Game Commission

Food and Agriculture, Director of

Forestry, Department of

Funeral Directors and Embalmers, State Board of

Geologists and Geophysicists, State Board of Registration for

Guide Dogs for the Blind, State Board of

Health Services, State Department of

Home Furnishings, Bureau of

Horse Racing Board, California

Insurance Commissioner

Labor Commissioner

Landscape Architects, State Board of
Medical Quality Assurance, Board of,
Medical Quality Review Committees and Examining Committees
Mental Health, State Department of
Motor Vehicles, Department of
Navigation and Ocean Development, Department of
Nursing, Board of Registered
Nursing Home Administrators, Board of Examiners of
Optometry, State Board of
Osteopathic Examiners of the State of California, Board of
Pharmacy, California State Board of
Public Employees' Retirement System, Board of Administration of the
Real Estate, Department of
Electronic and Applicance Repair, Bureau of
Resources Agency, Secretary of the
San Francisco, San Pablo and Suisun, Board of Pilot Commissioners for the Bays of
Savings and Loan Commissioner
School Districts
Shorthand Reporters Board, Certified
Social Services, State Department of
Statewide Health Planning and Development, Office of
Sructural Pest Control Board
Tax Preparer Program, Administrator
Teacher Preparation and Licensing, Commission for
Teachers' Retirement System, State
Transportation, Department of, acting pursuant to the State Aeronautics Act
Veterinary Medicine, Board of Examiners in
Vocational Nurse and Psychiatric Technician Examiners of the State of California, Board of
Water Resources, Department of

Table 4-3
Central Panel Operations: Reported Number of
Contested Cases Filed and Number of ALJs

	Total contested cases filed per month in 1980	Number of ALJs
California	333	24 plus 1 deputy director
Colorado	833	14[3]
Florida	233[1]	18 plus 1 assistant director
Massachusetts	83-100	11
Minnesota	83[2]	13 ALJs[4]
		19 compensation judges (added in 1981)[5]
New Jersey	750	45 plus 2 deputy directors
Tennessee	33	5

NOTES
Source: Interviews with directors, September-October, 1980.
1. Approximately 5% of the filings involve determining the validity of agency rules.
2. Approximately 16% of the filings involve rulemaking proceedings. With the 1981 addition of 19 compensation judges, the monthly caseload increased by 500 cases per month.
3. One ALJ is employed strictly for hearing cases where there is a conflict of interest involving the Division of Hearing Officers.
4. Ten attorneys are under contract to serve as ALJs as needed if the workload cannot be handled by current staff.
5. Compensation judges preside exclusively over contested workers' compensation cases.

Table 4-4
Central Panel Systems: Budgets

	Approx. 1980 operating budget	Salary range of directors in 1980	Salary range of ALJs in 1980
California	$3,500,000	$3,992 per month	Hearing Officer I: $3284-3973 per mo. Hearing Officer II:[3] $3443-4165 per mo.
Colorado	$510,000[1]	$2,584 per month	$1929-$2984 per month
Florida	$1,200,000	Figure not available	$2083-$3083 per month
Massachusetts	$320,000[2]	$2167-$2750 per month	Junior Hearing Officers:[4] $1073-$1289 per mo. Hearing Officers $1516-$1873 per mo.
Minnesota	$866,000	$3,333 per month	Hearing Examiner I:[5] $1707-$2109 per mo. Hearing Examiner II: $2109-$2814 per mo. Hearing Examiner III: $2434-$3010 per mo. Compensation Judge (since 1981): $3000 per month
New Jersey	$4,100,000	$4,000 per month	$2500-$3625 per month (entry level salaries—increases are based on performance evaluation results).
Tennessee	Figure not available	$1700-$2300 per month	$1540-$2200 per month

NOTES
1. Some expenses are the responsibility of personnel and labor departments which house some AJS.
2. 1979 figure.
3. The Hearing Officer II position involves more administrative responsibilities than Hearing Officer I.
4. Hired without trial experience. May be promoted to Hearing Officer.
5. Hearing Examiner I is a trainee position and may be promoted to Hearing Examiner II. Hearing Examiner III is required to spend 2/3 time hearing cases and to spend 1/3 time in supervisory duties.

Table 4-5
Central Panels: Responsibilities

California	Provide ALJs for contested hearings. Investigate various aspects of the administrative process. Publish the Administrative Law Bulletin—a digest of appellate court cases on administrative law and other articles. Provide ALJs to sit with agency personnel during formal peer review panels (ALJs serve to conduct the hearing, inform the agency of the law and how to apply it; agency executives render the decision and the ALJ writes the opinion).
Colorado	Provide ALJs for contested hearings.
Florida	Provide ALJs for contested hearings and for determining the validity of agency rules.
Massachusetts	Provide ALJs for contested hearings.
Minnesota	Provide ALJs for contested hearings and for rulemaking proceedings. Adopt procedural rules for rulemaking hearings, power plant siting and high voltage transmission line routing, and procedures for expedited hearings under the Revenue Recapture Act.
New Jersey	Provide ALJs for contested hearings. Office of Administrative Law develops rules for the process, and oversees filing and promulgating rules and regulations.
Tennessee	Provide ALJs for contested hearings. Hear agency rules disputes. Administrative Procedures Division staffs two legislative committees dealing with sunset and legislative oversight of rules review. Administrative Procedures Division is responsible for rules filings.

Table 4-6
How Cases Reach the Central Panels for Hearing

California	Process is initiated by the agency (the citizen does not have standing). A request for hearing is made of the Office of Administrative Hearings and, upon approval, the panel office sets a date for hearing.
Colorado	In social service cases, litigants request a hearing directly from the Department of Hearing Officers. The agency requests a hearing in other types of cases.
Florida	The process varies by type of case: *Majority of hearings:* person affected by agency action petitions that agency for a hearing. Upon deciding a hearing is warranted, the agency requests a hearing date from the DAH. *Rules challenges:* petition is filed directly with the Dept. of Administrative Hearings by any person substantially affected by a rule. *Involuntary commitment of persons to mental institutions:* Circuit Court initially commits patients for period of six months. At the expiration of that period, hospital may petition the DAH directly for hearing to determine if commitment order should continue.
Massachusetts	Agency petitions the Division of Hearing Officers for hearing. Exception: Rate Setting appeals are filed directly with the DHO by the provider of services. (The average litigant does not have standing to initiate a case.)
Minnesota	Agencies must request hearing. Exception: State employees may appeal directly to the Office of Administrative Hearings from disciplinary action.
New Jersey	The agency, upon determining that a claim represents a contested case, petitions the Office of Administrative Law for a hearing. (A litigant may not approach the DAL.)
Tennessee	The agency will call the Administrative Procedures Division to schedule a hearing date (notice of hearing will later by submitted to APD in writing). Litigants do not have jurisdiction to schedule a case.

Table 4-7
Directors' Profiles: A Sampling of Duties

Initially organized the central panel

Develop budget

Develop rules of procedure

Develop performance standards for ALJs

Develop library resources

Involved with hiring of ALJs

Evaluate ALJs

Review ALJ decisions

Oversee training of new ALJs

Oversee continuing education of ALJs

Assign cases to ALJs

Docket cases

Manage the office

Hire support staff

Consult with administrative agencies

Consult with the legislature

Hear cases

Table 4-8
Directors' Profile: Official Title

California	Director (California Gov't Code §11370.1)
Colorado	Director
Florida	Director (Florida Stat. Ann. §120.65 (1))
Massachusetts	Chief Hearings Officer (Mass. Ann. Laws Ch. 7 §4H)
Minnesota	Chief Hearing Examiner (Minn. Stat. Ann. §15.052 (subd. 1)).
New Jersey	Director (N. J. Stat. Ann. §52:14F-3)
Tennessee	Director

Table 4-9
Directors' Profile: Qualifications

California	Member of California Bar for 5 years; 2 years administrative experience as either a hearing officer or as a lawyer. "The director shall have the same qualifications as hearing officers...." (Cal. Gov't Code §11370.2 (b)).
Colorado	Attorney at law; If hiring within civil service system, 5 years experience. If hiring from outside system, 7 years experience. Experience must include management and litigation.
Florida	Member of Florida Bar for 5 years. (Fla. Stat. Ann. §120.65 (2)).
Massachusetts	Member of Massachusetts Bar; Massachusetts resident; substantial trial experience. (Mass. Ann. Laws Ch. 7 §4H).
Minnesota	"Learned in the Law." (attorney or legally educated) (Minn. Stat. Ann. §15.052 (subd. 1)).
New Jersey	Attorney at Law. (N. J. Stat. Ann. §52:14F-3).
Tennessee	Member of Tennessee Bar.

Table 4-10
Directors' Profile: Appointment

California	By governor with confirmation of senate. (Cal. Gov't Code §11370.2 (b)).
Colorado	By civil service system. (Competitive examination followed by a written test. Oral board is then given and the top three candidates are interviewed by director of the Dept. of Administration. If selection from outside Civil Service, there is one year probationary appointment leading to Civil Service status. (Source: Interview with director, September, 1980).
Florida	By majority vote of the governor and his cabinet of six sitting as the Administrative Commission; confirmation of the senate. (Fla. Stat.Ann. §120.65 (1)).
Massachusetts	By Secretary of Administration and Finance with the approval of the governor. (Mass. Ann. Laws Ch. 7 §4H).
Minnesota	By the governor with the advice and consent of the senate. (Minn. Stat. Ann. §15.052 (subd. 1)).
New Jersey	By the governor with the advice and consent of the senate. (N.J. Stat. Ann. §52:14F-3).
Tennessee	By the Secretary of State.

Table 4-11
Directors' Profile: Term of Office

California	At the discretion of the Governor
Colorado	No set term—Civil Service status (can be removed only "for cause")
Florida	At the discretion of the Administrative Commission
Massachusetts	At the discretion of the Secretary of Administration and Finance
Minnesota	Term ends June 30th of sixth calendar year after appointment (Minn. Stat. Ann. §15.052 (subd. 1))
New Jersey	Six years (N. J. Stat. Ann. §52:14F-3)
Tennessee	At the discretion of the Secretary of State

Table 4-12
Directors's Profile: Formal Methods of Evaluation and Removal

	Evaluation	Removal
California	None	At the discretion of the governor
Colorado	By the deputy director of the Department of Administration	Civil Service protection
Florida	None	At the discretion of the Administrative Commission
Massachusetts	None	At the discretion of the Secretary of Administration and Finance
Minnesota	None	Removal for cause (Minn. Stat. Ann. §15.052 (subd. 1)).
New Jersey	None	Removal for cause
Tennessee	None	None

Another type of jurisdiction is what we call "blanket Administrative Act coverage" (See Table 4-2). In Colorado, Florida, Minnesota, and New Jersey, the state APA delineates exceptions—agencies that do not have to utilize central pool ALJs. It is understood that all other agencies must use pool ALJs. The other type of jurisdiction is voluntary use of central panel services. A few agencies are required to use the pool in Massachusetts and Tennessee, but the majority of agencies have the discretion to decide whether to use the system. The director of the program in Massachusetts reports that every six months one new agency chooses to use the services of the pool hearing officers.[5]

The issue of mandatory versus voluntary jurisdiction relates to the objectives of a centralized situation. Proponents of a mandatory system claim that ALJs will be independent of agency influence only if agencies must utilize pool ALJs for all of their adjudications. An agency that can, at its option, use its own hearing officers will be free to consciously divide its hearing load between the two types of ALJs. This, say the proponents of mandatory jurisdiction, will destroy the appearance of justice that the central panel program seeks. Advocates of voluntary jurisdiction argue that because agency officials will feel less threatened by a voluntary use of pool ALJs, there will be fewer problems in implementing the central panel. As agency officials see the benefits of the system, an increasing number of agencies will begin to use it. In the end, they claim the same number of agencies will be using the panel and with fewer changeover problems. (Yet it is also possible that agency officials, not wishing to relinquish any control over agency operations, will never use the services of outside hearing officers.)

The newness of these systems and a lack of data prohibit conclusions about the impact of jurisdiction on central panel operations. The topic, nevertheless, has produced enough controversy to warrant its consideration in the 1981 revision of the Model State Administrative Procedure Act, which expressly provides for both types of jurisdiction.[6]

Organizational Structure

The panels also vary greatly as to caseload and the number of ALJs available. As shown in Table 4-3, the number of ALJs range from 45 in New Jersey to five in Tennessee. We also report in Table 4-3 the directors' estimation of the number of contested cases filed monthly. These statistics help illustrate the disparate nature of operations among the panels. A correspondingly large difference can be found when budgetary figures are compared in Table 4-4.

The responsibilities of central panels all include the providing of ALJs for contested hearings. But as we show in Table 4-5, panels in California, New Jersey, and Tennessee provide other types of services—ranging from staffing legislative committees in Tennessee to providing ALJs to sit with agency personnel during formal peer review panels in California. Directors in Florida, Minnesota, New Jersey, and Tennessee also report central panel ALJs are involved in the rulemaking process.

A significant area of similarity can be found in Table 4-6. The large majority of cases heard by pool ALJs result from requests for hearings made by the agencies. Only rarely (such as social service cases in Colorado and state employee discipline cases in Minnesota) can a private litigant approach the central panel for a hearing.

Directors of Central Panels

Each of the seven panels we studied was under the control of a director whose responsibilities varied among the states. While the jurisdiction of the central panel provides its general boundaries, it is the director who shapes the operating procedures of each panel. Cases are assigned to ALJs by the director and in Minnesota, New Jersey, Tennessee, Florida, Colorado, and California, directors' evaluations of ALJ performance bear directly upon salary increases. Directors are also integrally involved in the ALJ selection process in all seven states.[7] A list of these and other duties can be found in Table 4-7.

While we use the term "director" to refer to the individual responsible for central panel operations, the official term varies among the states (See Table 4-8). All current directors are lawyers (See Table 4-9) and were selected through a variety of procedures outlined in Table 4-10. Though the Colorado director is chosen through the civil service system, all other directors are appointed through the state political structure. Once appointed, directors are given administrative control over the operations. Each is responsible for budget development and general office management (See Table 4-7). Additionally, all directors are given the discretion to hear cases as administrative law judges. In all instances but California, directors have chosen to hear cases despite the fact that the procedure leading to their appointment is substantially different from the selection of other central panel ALJs.[8]

Tables 4-11 and 4-12 show the provisions for directors' term of office, evaluation, and removal. Only two states—Minnesota and New Jersey—provide a specific term of office. Both are six year terms, but a provision dealing with successorship distinguishes the two states. The successor of the current Minnesota director will receive a six-year term, even if the successor replaces a director whose term was not completed. If a vacancy occurs in New Jersey, a new director would be appointed only for the remainder of the old director's term.[9]

The position of director is critical to the integrity of the central panel operation. Because of their wide-ranging responsibilities, directors have made a substantial impact on the quality of ALJs, the extent to which pool ALJs will hear a variety of cases, and the degree to which these ALJs are separated from the agencies. Because of their visibility, directors also are in a position to affect the potentially stormy relationship between state agencies and the central panels.

The importance of the position, though, raises a potentially troubling issue. Although the central panel is supposed to eliminate bias, directors are selected by elected officials, and may then appear susceptible to influence from the official who nominated them. Current directors downplay this possibility. The California director, for example, notes that his appointment was "apolitical," that he and the governor who appointed him were members of different parties, and that other directors have served under several governors.[10] Tennessee gives the power of appointment to the Secretary of State, a constitutional office separate from the state's executive branch. Two states—Minnesota and New Jersey—give the director a six-year term—longer than the governor who appoints them.

Whether the process used to select directors will adversely affect the appearance of justice depends upon the role played by each director. Several directors during a recent workshop on central panels (sponsored by the American Judicature Society and the Administrative Conference of the U.S.) said their contact with the political system was an advantage. In effect, they saw their role as a buffer between state government and the decisionmaking independence of ALJs. A director familiar with and accepted by the political system, they said, can better resist attempts by a governor, for example, to interfere with the administrative process.[11]

NOTES

1. Clarkson, "The History of the California Administrative Procedure Act," 15 *The Hastings L.J.* 237 (1964).

2. *Id.*

3. *Id.*

4. Cal. Gov't. Code Sec. 11501.

5. Interview, September 1980.

6. National Conference of Commissioners on Uniform State Laws, Model State Administrative Procedure Act (1981 Revision). *See* Levinson, "The central panel system: a framework that separates ALJs from administrative agencies," 65 *Judicature* 236 (1981).

7. *See* Chapter 5.

8. For a discussion of the methods used to select central panel ALJs, *see* Chapter 5.

9. Interviews with Minnesota's Chief Hearing Examiner and New Jersey's director, September, 1980.

10. Interview with director of California central panel, September, 1980.

11. AJS/ACUS Workshop on Central Panel State Administrative Law Judge Systems, Chicago, Illinois, May 8, 1981.

5

The Role of the Administrative Law Judge Within the Central Panel

The administrative law judge has been at the forefront of change directed at both the federal and state administrative processes. When efforts were recently made in the Congress to change the tenure of federal ALJs and to institute a mandatory performance evaluation of ALJs, one of the rallying cries among the proponents of the status quo was that ALJs deserve the judicial independence granted to state and federal court judges.

Related to the notion of ALJ independence is the amount of expertise that an ALJ should bring to the hearing process. Those who see little need for expertise view ALJs as "generalists," administrative judges who are capable of hearing a variety of types of cases. Their critics subscribe to the view that administrative judges are present and are useful only because of their specialized expertise in one area and, therefore, should only hear one type of case.

The ALJ role has often been generally defined in terms of the required amounts of expertise and of independence. The two areas—expertise and independence—are related. According to some proponents of central pools, ALJ independence depends upon ensuring that ALJs are capable of hearing all kinds of cases. If the system assigns ALJs exclusively to one agency, it risks a bias among its ALJs that the central panel was devised to eliminate. Said one observer:

> When a judge possesses true expertise in a subject matter, a significant danger exists that conclusions may be reached on perceptions or information outside the record. This would be a manifestation of bias, and special efforts to avoid any resulting unfairness would be indicated.[1]

Others argue that the lack of specialized ALJ expertise leads to inefficiency. Rotating ALJs from agency to agency, they say, will not allow these administrative judges to acquire the expertise necessary to deal with highly complex cases in an effective and efficient manner.[2] These opponents also argue that ALJs without specific knowledge will have to be educated by the parties and will consequently be subject to manipulation.

Yet acquiring information from the parties has always been part of judging.

> Most of the time, the best judge is the individual who possesses the capacity by way of insight, temperament and knowledge to make fair and constructive use of the expertise of others. A judge should not usually be the source of the information, technical or otherwise, upon which a result is based.[3]

These two issues—evaluation and expertise—go to the heart of the ALJ role because they involve what ALJs do day-to-day. In this chapter, we will examine the ALJ role by first comparing qualifications for the position of ALJ, methods of recruitment, selection, evaluation, and removal. We will then look at the way central panel ALJs are assigned to cases, including the need for specialized expertise.

Title, Qualifications, and Selection Process

Table 5-1 reports the official title of what we refer to as administrative law judges. The title given to administrative law judges has been a point of debate in the past. At the federal level, the term "hearing examiner," as used in the federal APA, was changed by the Congress in 1972 to administrative law judge. The change, strongly supported by the American Bar Association, was not achieved without a fight. This debate might be considered by some as cosmetic but to others this change to the term ALJ meant that the federal government recognized the judicial-like qualities of these administrative hearing examiners. Among the seven panels, only two, California and New Jersey, refer to their presiding officers as administrative law judges. Yet as the director in New Jersey said to us, "The term [ALJ] has some significance but it's the function that's really important. It doesn't make any difference what you call them. It's the authority they've got and the level of quality with which they exercise it—that's really significant."[4]

The qualifications of ALJs, their recruitment, as well as their selection and evaluation, vary greatly among the states. Some aspects of state panels closely resemble the federal system. Other aspects, however, are much more simplistic. In all states but New Jersey, central panel ALJs must be lawyers (See Table 5-2) and the majority of these attorneys worked for governmental units prior to becoming an ALJ (Table 5-5). Methods used to recruit administrative law judges can be found in Table 5-3. Interestingly, although directors inform us that substantial effort goes into recruiting ALJs through formal means, over half of all central panel ALJs responding to our questionnaire report that they were recruited through informal means.[5]

The issue of selecting ALJs has been an important topic at the federal level. That system has been described as a merit system, although its critics point to what they consider to be arbitrary and discriminatory provisions of the process—a process which seems to favor candidates with a background of government employment.[6] Among the central panels, the ALJ selection procedures all include a key role performed by the director. It is the director who either makes the final decision or recommends a candidate be chosen. Other aspects of the processes vary widely among the states. The selection procedure itself ranges from a relatively simple review process in states such as Florida, Massachusetts, and Tennessee, to elaborate and intensive procedures in states such as California, Colorado, Minnesota, and New Jersey. In these latter states, oral and written examinations are included. The California and Minnesota systems somewhat resemble the techniques employed by the federal process (See Table 5-4).[7]

In Tables 5-5 and 5-6, we report the demographic characteristics of the ALJs chosen through the selection process at the state level. As we said earlier, the majority of central panel ALJs were formerly government employees. But among those who came from law firms, the majority practiced in smaller firms and virtually none came from large law firms. Another distinguishing factor among our respondents was that the majority of central panel ALJs received their highest academic degree from a school in the same state in which they are currently employed. This percentage ranges from 95 per cent in California to 50 per cent in both New Jersey and Tennessee. Thus, the corps of central panel ALJs tend to be a product of the state they now serve.

Evaluation and Removal

Two hotly debated topics at the federal level have been the issues of term of office and provisions for evaluation and removal of administrative law judges.[8] A specific term of office exists only in the state of New Jersey, among the states that we have studied. The term is five years plus the period of time until the appointment of a successor. In all other states, there is no term of office and in California, Colorado, and Minnesota, administrative law judges enjoy civil service status. Florida requires a six-month probationary period during which hearing officers may be fired without cause, but they then acquire permanent employment status. The least protection offered to administrative law judges can be found in Massachusetts where removal is at the discretion of the chief hearing officer. No employment protection is provided (See Table 5-7).

Opponents of any type of evaluation of administrative law judges look to general jurisdiction judges as examples. According to their view, other judges are not evaluated formally because they must enjoy absolute independence if the judicial system is to remain impartial. For the same reasons, opponents of evaluation state that administrative law judges should not be evaluated.

In 1978, this issue spilled into the federal courts in a Second Circuit Court of Appeals case, *Nash v. Califano*.[9] There, a federal appellate court judge ruled that a federal Social Security ALJ had standing to bring suit against his agency for infringing his decisional independence in violation of the federal APA. The Social Security Administration had imposed a quantitative evaluation system upon their ALJs. The case was remanded to the lower court for consideration.

Proponents of the evaluation of ALJs claim that administrative law judges should be accountable for their actions and accountability, in their view, can be accomplished through the evaluation of ALJ performance. Thus, evaluation of ALJs is part of the duties of the directors. For the most part, these evaluations take the form of annual reviews which in most states bear upon salary increases granted to ALJs. However, two evaluation systems are worthy of special note.

The New Jersey system of evaluation (which emanated from a report issued by a committee of the New Jersey Supreme Court regarding evaluation of state judges) includes measures of productivity, conduct, and quality. It is a rigorous system whose results bear directly upon increases in pay granted to New Jersey ALJs. These is no automatic pay increase in New Jersey with the exception of cost of living benefits granted by the legislature. Instead, the director has the discretion of increasing an ALJ's salary up to 10 per cent or decreasing it up to five per cent based upon the evaluation system.[10]

In Minnesota, salary ranges are based on minimums and maximums. Salaries are based solely on the results of ALJ performance evaluation— increases range from 0-8% for satisfactory performance, 0-11% for above average performance, and 0-14% for outstanding performance. There are no cost-of-living adjustments nor guaranteed increases each year. We summarize these and other systems of evaluating central panel ALJs in Table 5-8.

New Jersey and Minnesota are thus very different from the states of California and Massachusetts, which increase an ALJ's salary on an auto-matic basis under the states' salary schedule. We summarize methods used to make promotion and salary decisions in Table 5-9. In Tennessee, salary increases are made at the discretion of the Secretary of State, who utilizes the annual evaluation prepared by the director. A hybrid sort of system exists in Minnesota where, although the ALJs and workers' com-pensation judges are in the civil service system, their salaries are not established by that system. ALJs' salaries are based on performance only (as we discussed earlier) and compensation judges' salaries are established by the legislature.[11] What is clear after examining evaluation and salary issues among the states is that in the majority of states, directors have a great deal of power in regard to the financial well-being and status of their ALJs.

Evaluation is very much a part of most central panel ALJs' careers. But does evaluation affect their decisionmaking independence? Using a questionnaire mail survey, we asked central panel ALJs whether the presence of a performance evaluation system would jeopardize their independence. Table 5-10 shows that more ALJs disagree or strongly disagree with the idea that performance evaluation would jeopardize their independence than those who agree. This is somewhat surprising in light of a fairly uniform opposition to performance evaluation on the part of federal ALJs.[12]

We tabulate the responses to our question involving performance evaluation by state and report the results in Table 5-11. The results varied substantially by state, suggesting that state central panel ALJ viewpoints are fashioned by their individual experience. Note, then, that in the state of New Jersey where evaluation is among the most rigorous of any of the states, nearly three-fifths of the responding ALJs stated that the presence of a mechanism evaluating their performance would not jeopardize their independence.

The Need for Specialized Expertise

Still another area of conflict has to do with the requirement of specialized expertise. As we pointed out earlier, this issue is at the heart of the generalist v. specialist debate, which in turn bears upon the role of the judge as agency employee or judicial figure. Among other questions involving work-related viewpoints, we asked central panel ALJ respondents whether an ALJ should have specific expertise in the areas over which he or she presides. We report the results in Table 5-10. The results were split almost evenly between those agreeing and disagreeing that ALJs should have specific expertise. This split is of particular note in light of the responses to other questions about how a central panel affects an ALJ's work (Table 5-12). Central panel ALJ respondents are overwhelmingly satisfied with the central panel approach. They report that they are better insulated from agency influence and that they do not experience too much variety in the cases coming before them.

In Table 5-13, we tabulate the question concerning ALJs' specific expertise by state. Again, as with the independence question, the results vary substantially by state, implying that ALJs' viewpoints have more to do with their day-to-day experiences than with a more general global view—including the way in which the panel is operated. We therefore asked the directors whether ALJs are assigned to cases on the basis of specialized expertise.

First, it must be noted that directors do not have full discretion in this regard. The states of New Jersey, Minnesota, and Florida provide that ALJs must be assigned on the basis of specialized expertise. As Table 5-14 shows, assignment is done on a case-by-case basis in all but two states. In Colorado, an ALJ is assigned to an agency for extended periods of time and in New Jersey, the ALJ is assigned to two or more agencies for an extended period of time. During the time that they are assigned to these agencies, however, they are assigned on a case-by-case basis.[13] Insofar as expertise is related to the assignment process, it is a factor.

From our interviews, we found that directors generally seek to assign ALJs with specialized expertise to cases where that expertise can be utilized but to ultimately have a corps of centralized ALJs that is expert in a variety of cases. For example, the director in Colorado answered affirmatively when asked; "Is the ALJ assigned with his or her expertise in mind?" But she further stated that she wants to "eventually train all hearing officers to hear all types of cases."

> If a hearing officer does one kind of case for a long period of time, he will have a tendency to stop listening. Moving the hearing officers around brings freshness to the system. Lawyers complain that they have to train the judges on the law, but this is what lawyers should do.[14]

The issue of expertise also relates to the complexity of cases. The director in Massachusetts assigns ALJs with expertise in mind "when there are particularly complex cases.... [O]therwise, the hearing officers are broken into all types of hearings and are rotated regularly."[15] We summarize directors' responses in Table 5-15. One system, however, that is structured differently in regard to expertise is the Office of Administrative Hearings in Minnesota. Their central panel is organized into three areas for the purposes of case assignment and supervision: (1) utilities and transportation law, (2) environmental law, and (3) all other cases. In general, the director in Minnesota is following a legislative mandate which requires the director to assign on the basis of expertise. From his statements, though, he feels that this is the desired approach. In fact, he calls it "the only sensible way to operate."[16]

Table 5-1
Administrative Law Judges' Profile: Official Title

California	Hearing Officer (Cal. Gov't. Code §11502 (Administratively changed to Administrative Law Judge in 1975)
Colorado	Hearing Officer (Colo. Rev. Stat. §24-30-1001)
Florida	Hearing Officer (Fla. Stat. Ann. §120.65(2))
Massachusetts	Hearing Officer (Mass. Ann. Laws Ch. 7 §4H)
Minnesota	Hearing Examiner (Minn. Stat. Ann. §15.052(1)); Compensation Judge (for those hearing contested workers' compensation cases exclusively. Minn. Stat. Ann. §15.052(subd. 1))
New Jersey	Administrative Law Judge (N.J. Stat. Ann. §52:14F-4)
Tennessee	Administrative Judge (Tenn. Code Ann. §4-5-321)

Table 5-2
Administrative Law Judges' Profile: Qualifications

California	Member of California Bar for 5 years; 2 years administrative experience (Cal. Gov't. Code §11502).
Colorado	Attorney at law; Member of Colorado Bar (Colo. Rev. Stat. §24-30-1003(2)); 5 years experience if hired from outside civil service system.
Florida	Attorney at Law and Member of Florida Bar for 5 years (Fla. Stat. Ann. §120.65(2)).
Massachusetts	Attorney at law; 2 years trial experience (Mass. Ann. Laws Ch. 7 §4H).
Minnesota	"Learned in the law" (interpreted by the Chief Hearing Examiner as meaning an attorney) Minn. Stat. Ann. §15.052(3). "Demonstrated knowledge administrative procedure and free of any political or economic association that would impair their ability to function officially in a fair and objective manner." Minn. Stat. Ann. §15.052(subd. 1). Compensation judges must be "learned in the law and free of any political or economic association that would impair their ability to function officially in a fair and objective manner and must have demonstrated knowledge of workers' compensation laws." Minn. Stat. Ann. §15.052(1).
New Jersey	Attorney at law in New Jersey or any persons who are not attorneys at law, but who, in the opinion of the Governor or the Director are qualified in the field of administrative law, administrative hearings, and proceedings in subject matter relating to the hearing functions of a particular state agency. A full time ALJ shall not hold other employment. (N.J. Stat. Ann §52:14F-5(1)).
Tennessee	Learned in the law as evidenced by being licensed to practice by the courts of Tennessee (Tenn. Code Ann. §4-5-321(2)).

Table 5-3
Administrative Law Judges' Profile: How ALJs Said They Were Recruited

	General newspaper advertisement	Legal publication	State employment bulletin	Informal means
California (N=18)	0%	38.9%	16.7%	44.4%
Colorado (N=9)	22.2%	0%	22.2%	55.6%
Florida (N=8)	12.5%	50.0%	0%	37.5%
Massachusetts (N=8)	0%	25.0%	0%	75.0%
Minnesota (N=11)	0%	18.2%	9.1%	72.7%
New Jersey (N=14)	7.1%	35.7%	0%	57.1%
Tennessee (N=2)	0%	0%	0%	100%
All States (N=70)	5.7%	28.6%	8.6%	57.1%

Table 5-4
Administrative Law Judges' Profile: Selection Process

California

Each applicant is given oral and written examinations by a panel composed of a representative of the Office of Administrative Hearings (OAH), a representative of the state personnel Board and a member of the public. Panelists evaluate the applicant and a ranking is established on the basis of the resulting scores. The ranks are based on percentiles and those who place in the top 3 percentiles are eligible for appointment. Note that additional points are automatically given for prior state service.

When a position opens, the Director of OAH advises all persons in the top three ranks. All interested candidates are interviewed by the Director who is usually joined by senior hearing officers. Applicants are probed on writing skills, ability to communicate, and demeanor. The Director makes the final hiring decision.

Colorado

Applications are screened by the Department of Administration to determine if minimum qualifications are met. There must be evidence of sufficient trial experience and background to be familiar enough with procedural rules to conduct a hearing. An oral board is then administered to the applicant by a performing or retired hearing officer, a lawyer with expertise in the area for which the hearing officer is sought, and a third person. The oral board grades the exams.

The Director of the Division of Hearing Officers interviews the top 3 applicants. Also present is a representative from the agency where the prospective hearing officer will hear cases on the first assignment. The Director makes the final decision with approval of the Executive Director of the Department of Administration (Colo. Rev. Stat. §24-30-1003(1)).

Florida

Applications are reviewed by the Director of the Division of Administrative Hearings. The current Director looks for a distinguished academic background and experience. Expertise is not a criterion. The final decision is made by the Director.

Massachusetts

The Chief Hearing Officer of the Division of Hearing Officers reviews resumes and writing samples from each of the applicants and interviews them. The Chief Hearing Officer then makes the hiring decision.

Minnesota

The Department of Personnel administers and grades a competitive examination. Points are also given if certain requirements are met. These include being admitted to the Minnesota Bar (or a state bar having similar requirements), being out of law school 5 years, having been involved in trial work and/or administrative hearings. Other sources of points include involvement in rule making hearings and veterans (and disabled veterans) preference. The Chief Hearing Examiner (CHE) receives the names of the top 10 candidates, who in turn, are notified of their status and asked to submit samples of their legal writing. Supervisors (Hearing Examiner III's) conduct interviews with those applying, and recommends "2 or 3" to the CHE. The CHE interviews these candidates and makes the decision to hire.

New Jersey

As of 1980, the Director of the Office of Administrative Law had the power to appoint temporary ALJs. The Director used this power to acquire the ALJs needed to begin operations. (The same system continued to be used.) The Director reviews the credentials of candidates and interviews them. Those hired by the Director are appointed on a temporary basis with final employment depending upon the results of performance evaluation. These results are given to the governor who makes the final decision to hire upon recommendation of the Director. As of 1982, "Permanent administrative law judges shall be appointed by the Governor with the advice and consent of the Senate to initial terms of 1 year.... First reappointment of a judge after this initial term shall be by the Governor for a term of 4 years.... Subsequent reappointments of a judge shall be by the Governor with the advice and consent of the Senate to terms of 5 years.... (N.J. Stat. Ann. §52:14F-4).

Tennessee

The Secretary of State is responsible for hiring but the decision is made upon recommendation of the Director, Administrative Procedures Division. The APD selects one or two applicants and sends them to the Secretary of State for a final interview.

Table 5-5
Selected Characteristics of Central Panel ALJ Respondents

Question:	Attorneys (N=72)	Percent	N
What was your occupation prior to serving as an ALJ in the central panel? (Note: Seven respondents were not attorneys.)	Solo practice	11.1%	(8)
	Small firm (2-10)	16.7	(12)
	Medium firm (11-30)	4.2	(3)
	Large firm (30 or more)	1.4	(1)
	Government	45.8	(33)
	ALJ	20.8	(15)
How many years have you been an ALJ with your central panel office?	Mean = 4.1 Median = 8.4		
Does your current position as an ALJ represent financial improvement or financial sacrifice when compared to your previous position?	Financial sacrifice	22.1%	(19)
	About the same	32.6	(28)
	Financial improvement	45.3	(39)
How did you learn of the vacancy for your current position?	General circulation newspaper ad	5.7%	(4)
	Legal newspaper or magazine	28.6	(20)
	State Employment Bulletin	8.6	(6)
	Informal means	57.1	(40)
Item:			
Percent of ALJ respondents receiving highest academic degree in the state of current employment:	Educated in state	69.0%	(60)
	Educated out of state	31.0	(27)

Table 5-6
Selected Characteristics of Central Panel ALJ Respondents by State

	California (N=21)	Colorado (N=7)	Florida (N=9)
Prior Occupation[*]			
Solo practice	14.3%	28.6%	0 %
Small firm (2-10)	19.0	14.3	11.1
Medium firm (11-30)	4.8	0	11.1
Large firm (30 or more)	0	0	11.1
Government attorney	52.4	42.9	44.4
ALJ	9.5	14.3	22.2
Years with central panel agency (mean)	9.1	3.7	2.6
Education Per cent of ALJ respondents receiving highest academic degree in the state of current employment	95.2	50.0	72

Massachusetts (N=8)	Minnesota (N=10)	New Jersey (N=22)	Tennessee (N=2)	
25.0%	0%	6.7%	0 %	
12.5	10.0	20.0	50.0	
0	0	6.7	0	
0	0	0	0	
50.0	40.0	40.0	50.0	
12.5	50.0	26.7	0	
2.4	3.5	1.9	2.0	
88.9	63.6	50.0	50.0	

*All respondents were attorneys except seven ALJs in New Jersey.

Table 5-7

Administrative Law Judges' Profile:

Term of Office and Removal Provisions

	Term of Office	Removal
California	No specific term (civil service status)	Civil Service procedure—removal for cause.
Colorado	No specific term (civil service status)	Civil Service procedure—removal for cause.
Florida	No specific term—Career Service System (6 month probationary period during which hearing officers may be fired without cause. They then acquire permanent employment status.)	Following a 6 month probationary period, removal for cause.
Massachusetts	No specific term	Removal at the discretion of the Chief Hearing Officer.
Minnesota	No specific term	Civil Service procedure: Following a 6 month probationary period, removal for cause.
New Jersey	Five years (and until the appointment of a successor) (N.J. Stat. Ann. §52:14F-4)	Removal for cause.
Tennessee	No specific term	Removal at the discretion of the Director.

Table 5-8
Administrative Law Judges' Profile: Evaluation

California
An annual review is prepared by the Director. In addition, Senior ALJs periodically review decisions of ALJs they supervise.

Colorado
Annual performance planning and review by the Director.

Florida
Annual review by the Director.

Massachusetts
Informal. Director observes hearings and reviews written decisions.

Minnesota
Annual review by the Chief Hearing Examiner.

New Jersey
Elaborate system of evaluation emanating from a report issued by a committee of the New Jersey Supreme Court regarding evaluation of state judges.
The document stressed three areas of importance: productivity, conduct, and quality.
• Several sets of statistics concerning case dispostions are used by the Director to measure productivity.
• Conduct is evaluated by a series of questionnaires sent confidentially to attorneys, litigants, and others involved in matters before the ALJs.
• Quality is measured through these questionnaires and by the Directors' review of a sample of ALJ decisions rendered during the six month evaluation period.
The Director compiles the results of the three-pronged system and generates an evaluation every six months.

Tennessee
Annual evaluation by the Director.

Table 5-9
Administrative Law Judges' Profile: Promotion and Salary Decisions

California
Salary increases are based on Civil Service procedures which require an annual evaluation report.

Colorado
Civil Service System: Automatic 5 per cent salary increase annually. Note: Future raises for hearing officers will depend on performance planning and review.

Florida
Salary increases based on across the board pay raises that may be provided by the legislature and discretionary salary increases given by the Director (based in part on the Director's evaluation of hearing officer performance).

Massachusetts
Automatic salary increase under the State's salary schedule.

Minnesota
Appointments to Hearing Examiner I (a trainee position), Hearing Examiner II or Hearing Examiner III (a supervisory position) made by Chief Hearing Examiner from list of eligible names certified to the Office of Administrative Hearings by the Department of Employee Relations. Salaries based on results of ALJ performance evaluation. Increases range from 0-8% for satisfactory performance, 0-11% for above average performance, 0-14% for outstanding performance. There are no cost of living adjustments nor any yearly guaranteed increases. Compensation judges' salaries are set at $36,000 annually by the legislature and receive no guaranteed increases nor performance increases.

New Jersey
Salary ranges are tied to the performance evaluation system. The only automatic raises are cost of living increments that the legislature may provide. On the basis of the evaluation, ALJs receive two salary increments annually; they may receive as much as a 10 per cent increase or a 5 per cent decrease.

Tennessee
Salary increases at the discretion of the Secretary of State who utilizes the annual evaluation prepared by the Director.

Table 5-10
Viewpoints of Central Panel ALJ Respondents on Evaluation and Expertise

Statements:	Agree*	Undecided	Disagree**
The presence of a mechanism evaluating the overall performance of ALJs will jeopardize the independence of ALJs. (N=84)	28.9%	22.9%	48.2%
An ALJ should have specific expertise in the areas over which he/she presides. (N=87)	43.6	13.8	42.5

*Respondents answered "agree" or "strongly agree."
**Respondents answered "disagree" or "strongly disagree."

Table 5-11
Work-Related Attitudes of Central Panel ALJ Respondents by State
Issue: The presence of a mechanism evaluating the overall performance of ALJs will jeopardize the independence of ALJs.

	Agree	Undecided	Disagree
California (N=21)	19.0%	23.8%	57.1%
Colorado (N=10)	30.0	20.0	50.0
Florida (N=9)	44.4	44.4	11.1
Massachusetts (N=7)	28.6	14.3	57.1
Minnesota (N=11)	45.5	18.2	36.4
New Jersey (N=23)	26.1	17.4	56.5
Tennessee (N=2)	0.0	50.0	50.0

Table 5-12
Work-Related Viewpoints of Central Panel ALJ Respondents

Statements:	Strongly Agree	Agree	Undecided	Disagree	Strongly Disagree
An ALJ should be free to deviate from the central panel rules of hearing procedure if the situation necessitates. (N=86)	23.3%	45.3%	8.1%	17.4%	5.8%
ALJs are adequately compensated for their work. (N=86)	0	18.6	3.5	47.7	30.2
An ALJ's skills are utilized more effectively in a central panel system. (N=85)	45.9	41.2	7.1	4.7	1.2
ALJs in a central panel system experience too much variety in the cases coming before them. (N=86)	1.2	5.8	8.1	46.5	38.4
ALJs are under undue pressure to decide cases quickly. (N=86)	16.3	37.2	9.3	31.4	5.8
Agency officials still view ALJs as agency employees. (N=84)	7.1	21.4	15.5	39.3	16.7
If an ALJ is employed by a central panel, his/her decisions will be better insulated from inappropriate agency influence. (N=85)	57.6	32.9	4.7	2.4	2.4
A central panel ALJ whose office quarters are located within an agency will more likely be subject to inappropriate agency influence. (N=86)	36.0	40.7	14.0	8.1	1.2

Table 5-13

Work-Related Attitudes of Central Panel ALJ Respondents by State

Issue: An ALJ Should Have Specific Expertise In The Areas Over Which He/She Presides.

	Agree*	Undecided	Disagree**
California (N=21)	4.8%	14.3%	80.9%
Colorado (N=10)	70.0	20.0	10.0
Florida (N=10)	30.0	0.0	70.0
Massachusetts (N=9)	88.9	0.0	11.1
Minnesota (N=11)	63.7	27.3	9.1
New Jersey (N=24)	50.0	16.7	33.3
Tennessee (N=2)	0.0	0.0	100.0

*Respondents answered "agree" or "strongly agree."
**Respondents answered "disagree" or "strongly disagree."

Table 5-14

How Administrative Law Judges are Assigned: Case by Case or to One Agency for an Extended Time Period.

California
Case by case

Colorado
To assigned agency for extended period of time

Florida
Case by case (Beverage cases and Baker Act cases are one year assignments.)

Massachusetts
Case by case

Minnesota
Case by case

New Jersey
Assigned to two or more agencies for extended period of time; then assigned on a case by case basis

Tennessee
Case by case

Table 5-15

Administrative Law Judge Assignment: Expertise

California
ALJs with particular specialties will be assigned to cases where they may make use of their talents. No ALJ, however, is assigned to just one agency and ALJs are not hired with expertise as a criterion.

Colorado
ALJs assigned with expertise in mind, but they are rotated to train them to hear a variety of cases.

Florida
ALJs assigned with expertise in mind, but they are rotated to hear a variety of cases.

Massachusetts
ALJs assigned with expertise in mind, but they are rotated to hear a variety of cases. ALJs are not hired with expertise as a criterion.

Minnesota
ALJs organized into 3 divisions for the purpose of case assignment: 1) Utilities and transportation law, 2) Environmental law, 3) All other areas. An attempt is made to assign ALJs with expertise in the area to be heard.

New Jersey
ALJs assigned with expertise in mind. The expertise will not result in assignment to one agency exclusively.

Tennessee
ALJs are not generally assigned on basis of expertise, but this is a factor when a highly technical case is involved.

NOTES

1. Kestin, "Reform of the Administrative Process," 92 *New Jersey Lawyer* 35 (1980).
2. Riccio, "Due Process in Quasi-Judicial Administrative Hearings: Confining the Examiner to One Hat," 2 *Seaton Hall L.J.* 398 (1971).
3. Kestin, *supra* note 1.
4. Interview with director of New Jersey central panel, September 1980.
5. An example of learning of the job vacancy through informal means is learning of it from friends or contacts in the work-setting.
6. "Selective certification allows federal agencies to hire individuals with special skills or experience in a particular area." The result is that individuals possessing these special skills most commonly acquire them by working or practicing before the agency using selective certification to hire its ALJs. Thus, many within the federal corps of ALJs have backgrounds including government employment. Report by the Comptroller General of the U.S., *Management Improvements in the Administrative Law Process: Much Remains to be Done*, FPLD 79-44 (May 23, 1979), at 42.
7. ALJs are selected by the agencies from rosters prepared by the Office of Personnel Management (OPM). Agencies can normally choose each ALJ from among the top three names on the appropriate roster. However, under the system of selective certification, an agency can arrange with OPM to select an ALJ from among the top three candidates fulfilling special requirements pertaining to specialized expertise. To qualify for placement on the roster, one needs to receive a score of 80 on a 100-point scale consisting of points for experience, recommendations, writing ability, and performance at an oral interview. The process is scored by OPM personnel. "Administrative Law Judge," *Office of Personnel Management, Announcement No. 318* (October 1979).

For a two-part article on federal ALJ selection, *see* Mans, "Selecting the 'hidden judiciary:' how the merit process works in choosing administrative law judges," 63 *Judicature* 60, 130 (1979). *See also* Lubbers, "Federal Administrative Law Judges: A Focus on Our Invisible Judiciary," 3 *Admin. L. Rev.* 109 (1981). For an evaluation of the federal ALJ selection process, see Sharon, "Validation of the Administrative Law Judge Examination," Report to the Office of Personnel Management (June 1980). *See also* Sharon, "The Measure of an Administrative Law Judge," 19/4 *The Judges' J.* 20 (1980).

8. For an overview of legislative efforts in these matters, *see* note 35 of Chapter 2 and "Congress hears proposals for 'performance reviews' of ALJs," 63 *Judicature* 144 (1979).
9. 613 F.2d 10 (2d Cir. 1980).
10. Interview with director of New Jersey central panel, September 1980.
11. Interviews with Chief Hearing Examiner in Minnesota, September-October 1980.
12. Proposed legislation providing for evaluation of federal ALJ performance was vigorously opposed by all organizations of federal ALJs. *See* note 8 *supra*. One example of ALJ efforts to oppose the legislation was testimony before various Congressional committees. *See, e.g., Senate Committee on Governmental Affairs* 96th Cong., 1st Sess. (May 1979) (testimony of Judge William Fauver on behalf of the Federal Administrative Law Judges Conference).

For an overview of the evaluation issue, *see* Rosenblum, "Evaluation of Administrative Law Judges: Aspects of Purpose, Policy and Feasibility," a paper submitted to the Administrative Conference of the United States, February 1981 (cited with permission of author).

13. Interview with director of New Jersey central panel, September 1980.
14. Interview with director of Colorado central panel, September 1980.
15. Interview with director of Massachusetts central panel, September 1980.
16. Interview with Chief Hearing Examiner in Minnesota, September 1980. Minn. Stat. Ann. §15.052 (subd. 3).

6

The Hearing Process and the Central Panel

In Chapter 5, we looked at the structure of the ALJ role within the central panel, the variety in the ways that ALJs are recruited, selected, and evaluated in state systems, and the work-related viewpoints that central panel ALJs expressed to us concerning that role. In this chapter, we examine the role of the central panel ALJ in terms of the hearing process—the day-to-day work behavior of administrative law judges. Specifically, we focus on questionnaire survey results given to us by administrative law judges in the seven central panel states. First, we look at work-related activities as well as resources reportedly available to these administrative judges. Then we focus on the hearing process itself, including rules of procedure, and a description of the hearings. Next we consider the ways in which the ALJ role fits into the administrative process. Finally, we look at the authority of the ALJ, including the finality of their decisions and the approximate rate at which they are accepted by the agencies.

Work-related Activities and Resources

Tables 6-1, 6-2, and 6-3 deal with general work-related activities and resources available to central panel ALJs. Table 6-1 shows that in nearly two-thirds of the time ALJs spend on the job they either preside at formal hearings or write decisions. However, a significant amount of time, nearly 16 per cent, is spent in pretrial activities, whether it be pretrial preparation or conducting pre-hearing proceedings.

We also looked at work-related activities and resources available to central panel ALJs. For example, on the question of whether ALJs consult their colleagues for advice or information prior to a hearing, the great majority of state ALJs report that this occurs frequently or occasionally but over half report they infrequently or never make suggestions to agency officials about policy changes (See Table 6-2).

In Table 6-3, we report resources available to central panel ALJs. For example, over three-fifths of those reporting found their law library to be adequate but nearly the same number reported that resources in the form of policy briefings by agency officials not only did not exist but were unnecessary.

Over four-fifths of central panel ALJ respondents also found uniform rules of practice pertaining to hearings to be adequate. We note that the hearings conducted by pool ALJs are often guided by rules of procedure issued by the central panel itself. These rules take a variety of forms, each of which is described in Table 6-4. In most cases, these rules are not rigid and serve as guidelines, not strict requirements.

In virtually all cases, hearings in the states are public and are recorded either by audio recording equipment or by court reporter (See Table 6-5). In all cases, attorneys may represent litigants but attorneys are not assigned to represent indigents. Whether attorneys are present depends upon the type of proceeding. At the federal level, attorneys often are not present in Social Security hearings, for example, but are always present in proceedings associated with the regulatory agencies. This distinction between social welfare and regulatory proceedings is also the case in state proceedings. Table 6-6 lists the frequency with which types of cases are heard by central panel ALJ respondents. However, this table is misleading for central panel administrative judges in light of the variety of cases heard by them. Therefore, Table 6-7 shows the combinations of cases that ALJs reported they heard frequently. This is only a rough view for we present only those cases that our respondents reported that they heard frequently as opposed to occasionally or infrequently. Half of our respondents, then, report that they hear one type of case only, while half hear at least two types of cases frequently.

Another factor related to combinations of cases heard frequently by pool ALJs is the combination in which regulatory type proceedings are combined with benefits adjudication. At the federal level, these two types of cases represent different models of judicialization. Within the regulatory model, ALJs preside over adversarial proceedings in which attorneys argue their cases, often utilizing formalized rules of evidence and procedure. In contrast, Social Security adjudication is nonadversarial. Litigants often argue their own cases before the ALJs, who must balance the interests of the litigant, the government, and the public. Yet within the central panels approximately one-fifth of ALJ respondents state that the combination of cases they hear includes both regulatory and benefits types of adjudication.

The Role of the ALJ in the Hearing Process

The remainder of this chapter deals with hearing-related activities of the state administrative law judges, for these activities truly define the role of the ALJ. We begin with a look at a variety of behaviors that are part of the administrative hearing. In Table 6-8, we present some of these activities and the frequencies with which they occur.

The frequency of these activities will vary depending upon the types of cases heard by the ALJs, but Table 6-8 shows that administrative judicial officers engage in many of the same activities as federal and state judges. A large majority of ALJs conduct prehearing conferences, for example. An equally large majority of central panel administrative law judges never issue decisions orally and all respondents direct counsel to brief certain legal issues. In most cases, decisions rendered by administrative judges are written, and these decisions are reviewed by the agency.

Among the states we studied, ALJ decisions are in writing and there are standards involving the form of the decision. We list those standards in Table 6-9, and note that in each case findings of facts are considered crucial. Never is a conclusion of law considered sufficient for an acceptable ALJ decision. One goal of the central panel directors is to ensure that decisions comprise a complete record. In California, "one policy is that the decision should be written in language which would be understandable by a person of average intelligence who has some interest in the proceeding. The decision should be informative in addition to being comprehensible; findings of fact to cover all the facts, conclusions of law on all the points of law that come to bear, and a proposed decision that squares the two."[1]

Litigants may see the ALJ's decision prior to the time the agency issues its final order. The ALJ issues a decision and the litigant is allowed time to view the decision and to decide whether to appeal to the agency for another consideration (See Table 6-10). If appealed, agency officials consider the case and issue the final order. They may accept the ALJ decision, may modify it, or may reject it in its entirety.

In Table 6-11, we look at the finality of central panel administrative law judge decisions to explore the authority of ALJs in the central panels. We see that in all states under study the ALJ decisions are generally recommended decisions, although in certain instances decisions are final. However, as pointed out in Table 6-12, the majority, sometimes as high as 95 per cent of the decisions, are accepted by the agencies as written or accepted with modifications. Thus, central panel ALJs are vested with a large amount of responsibility.

The final step is to catalog ALJ decisions. In most cases this process, while formalized on the federal court and state court levels, is done informally among the state administrative systems (See Table 6-13). As these systems become more sophisticated in their retrieval practices, some directors of central panel systems feel that precedent will become more binding in the future.

Acquiring Guidance from Agencies

The variety of cases heard by central panel ALJs coupled with their physical separation from the agencies has led some commentators to question whether ALJs can acquire the agency guidance they need as to the meaning of agency policies. They also ask to what extent agency policies are binding on ALJs who are no longer directly employed by the agency.

The processes through which ALJs are made aware of agency policies vary greatly among the states. Administrative judges must be made knowledgeable of agency policies while retaining adequate distance from agency personnel. California, for example, once allowed agencies to write their policies in secret documents that were available to the ALJs, who were presumed to rely upon these policies. The advantage of this system was that it produced consistent interpretation, "but had the disadvantage of being a unilateral ex parte communication."[2] The new director eliminated this system and asked agencies to present new documents only if they had been made public. He reports that approximately one-half of the agencies have reacted positively to this new system.

A similar public policy requirement exists in New Jersey—only policies that are matters of public record are allowed to be used by administrative law judges there.[3] And similarly, in Massachusetts, all agency regulations are on file and administrative notice is taken of them. In Minnesota, while the office of administrative hearings is not prohibited from using agency rules that are not public, ALJs can only use agency information that it has requested by letter from the agency which is served. The communication is served on all parties and is never done ex parte.[4]

The prohibition on ex parte communications between ALJs and agencies also exists in the Tennessee system. The distinguishing feature of this system, however, is that the Administrative Procedures Division also staffs a government operations committee, which exercises legislative oversight of agency rules. Thus, Tennessee agency rules are both filed with the central panel and analyzed by central panel hearing officers. The administrative judges here not only have the advantage of having agency rules without ex parte communications but also are integrally involved in their formulation.[5]

The question of whether central panel ALJs are able to acquire agency guidance relates to how the interaction of agencies with ALJs affects ALJ independence. The answer is related to the very nature of the hearing process. That is to say, when cases are clearly supported by or in violation of agency rulings and regulations, those cases do not come to hearing. The cases that are heard by ALJs are in a "gray" area where agency policy demands interpretation. The ALJs then are faced with whether the conflict they are supposed to resolve falls somewhere within the spectrum of interpretations associated with each agency policy.

The Binding Effect of Agency Policies

Yet there are some clear and differing standards among the states concerning just how binding agency policies are on administrative law judges. In Minnesota, for example, an agency must establish a policy by rule. According to the director,

> Once established, and the rule is in effect, the Office of Administrative Hearings is bound to follow that rule. Only the courts may find a rule illegal; a rule may not be challenged in a hearing.[6]

In instances where there are "gray areas of policy that are not defined, the hearing examiner must make recommendations on what the policy should be. This is where decisions are and should be recommendations."[7] Thus, in the Minnesota system, the ALJs are given discretion to interpret agency policy only where the agency has been unclear in defining its position.

Directors generally report that their ALJs will be bound by public agency regulations but not by interpretations of regulations issued by the agencies. The Administrative Procedures Division in Tennessee will follow the statutes or rules promulgated by the agency but will not be bound by agency argument.

> When you reach the stage of a hearing, you are usually in a gray area which the statute doesn't spell out exactly and neither do rules and that's why you have a hearing, so the Administrative Procedures Division is not bound by the agency interpretation of what their policy is or what the legislature intended.[8]

Similarly in Massachusetts, the Division of Hearing Officers will "construe regulations very strictly without regard to agency policy."[9] In Florida, the Division of Administrative Hearings uses "the agency interpretations of their statutes or rules as persuasive but not binding." As a practical matter, hearing officers are "probably not greatly influenced by agency interpretations simply because it's the agency interpretation."[10]

The central panels we have studied have gone to great lengths to ensure a separation between the central panel and the agencies. This is clear, but an equally critical issue is the extent to which ALJs are bound by the information they do receive from the agencies. From the discussions we have had with directors, the answer to that question depends largely on the formality with which agencies promulgate their policies. For the most part, rules and regulations are considered binding by ALJs.

Yet agency policies, even when promulgated through the rulemaking function, leave a large amount of room for interpretation. It is this agency interpretation that is never considered binding by pool ALJs. Therefore, the role of the ALJ, insofar as his or her relationship to agency policy is concerned, is shaped by agency actions. To the extent that the clarity of agency policies varies from one type of case to another, the ALJ role will differ as well. That role cannot be defined in isolation of the agencies the ALJs are meant to serve.

Table 6-1
Work-Related Activities of Central Panel ALJ Respondents

Question:	Mean	Median
How much of the total time spent doing your job is devoted to the following activities? (N=87)		
Pretrial preparation (reading, researching)	9.4%	9.8%
Conducting prehearing conferences and negotiations	6.5	5.1
Presiding at formal hearings	31.7	29.9
Writing decisions	33.8	33.1
Travel	6.5	5.1
Administrative duties	9.8	5.5
Other hearing-related activities	2.4	0.2

Table 6-2
Reported Work-Related Activities of Central Panel ALJs

	Frequently	Occasionally	Infrequently or Never
Read decisions of other ALJs (N=87)	55.2%	34.5%	10.3%
Read final agency decisions or opinions (N=86)	65.1	32.6	2.3
Read industry publications or commercial services (N=85)	9.4	35.3	55.3
Consult other ALJs for advice or information prior to hearing (N=86)	40.7	47.7	11.6
Consult other ALJs while case is pending (N=86)	26.7	45.3	27.9
Request drafts of decisions from your law clerk (N=75)	5.3	22.7	72.0
Talk with individual members of the private bar about agency procedures (N=87)	3.4	46.0	50.6
Make suggestions to agency officials about policy changes (N=87)	3.4	41.4	55.2
Make suggestions to agency officials about procedural changes (N=87)	5.7	44.8	49.4
Disqualify yourself from hearing a case (N=86)	0.0	29.1	70.9
Attend professional meetings or seminars (N=87)	18.4	72.4	9.2
Wear a robe during a hearing (N=82)	*	*	*

*No respondents currently wear judicial robes but respondents in New Jersey report that they will soon begin to wear robes during hearings.

Table 6-3
Reported Resources Available to Central Panel ALJs

	Adequate	Inadequate	Do not have but desirable	Do not have and unnecessary
Law library (N=85)	61.2%	37.6%	1.2%	0.0%
Personal law clerk (N=83)	0.0	2.4	38.6	59.0
Shared law clerk (N=85)	23.5	8.2	41.2	27.1
Personal secretarial assistance (N=80)	12.5	2.5	46.2	38.7
Shared secretarial assistance (N=83)	63.9	30.1	4.8	1.2
Subscriptions to legal periodicals or commercial services (N=83)	47.0	37.3	10.8	4.8
Regular policy briefings by agency officials (N=85)	15.3	12.9	11.8	60.0
Hearing manual for ALJs (N=84)	32.1	8.3	41.7	17.9
Technical assistance by designated staff member (N=81)	30.9	6.2	22.2	40.7
Index of prior ALJ decisions (N=85)	34.1	16.5	36.5	12.9
Uniform rules of practice for all hearings (N=85)	81.0	7.1	6.0	6.0
Magnetic media typewriters or other modern office equipment (N=84)	50.0	13.1	27.4	9.5
Financial support for attending continuing education seminars, meetings (N=84)	35.7	44.0	19.0	1.2

Table 6-4

Hearing Process: Rules of Procedure

California	State Administrative Manual (behavior and conditions of employment for all state employees); Forms Book (for the assistance of the ALJ); Policy statements from agencies (guidelines from which ALJs may deviate); Operation Memos (relate to hearing procedures, e.g., how much time to give a lawyer to submit a written argument, who swears in a witness, etc.). California Administrative Procedure Act.
Colorado	Administrative Procedure Act §24-14-101 *et. seq.* Rules of Civil Procedure For District Courts of Colorado (as far as practicable)
Florida	Ch. 28-5 Fla. Admin. Code Model Rules of Procedure
Massachusetts	Informal and formal rules of procedure drafted by a former Director, Division of Hearing Officers. Rules of Practice and Procedure, 801 CMR 1.00
Minnesota	9 Minn. Code of Agency Rules §2.101 *et. seq.*, 2.201 *et. seq.*, 2.301 *et. seq.*, 2.401 *et. seq.*, 2.501 *et. seq.*
New Jersey	Uniform Administrative Procedure Rules of Practice
Tennessee	Uniform Rules §1360-1-7

Table 6-5
Hearing-Related Activities: Are Hearings Public, Are Hearings
Recorded, and Is There a Right to Counsel?

	All hearings public	All hearings recorded	Right to counsel
California	Yes	Yes	Attorneys may represent litigants in all cases but attorneys are never assigned.
Colorado	Yes	Yes	Same
Florida	Yes	Yes	Same*
Massachusetts	Controlled by statute. Qualified parties have the right to request hearings be public	Yes	Same
Minnesota	Yes	Yes	Same
New Jersey	Yes	Yes	Same
Tennessee	Yes	Yes	Same

*Note: Public defenders represent indigents in Baker Act (civil commitment) proceedings.

Table 6-6
Types of Cases Heard by Central Panel Administrative Law Judges

	Frequently	Occasionally	Infrequently or never
Licensing, permit, or certificate applications, suspensions, or revocations (N=86)	74.4%	22.1%	3.5%
Ratemaking or valuations (N=81)	17.3	19.8	63.0
Rulemaking, regulations (N=80)	12.5	21.2	66.2
Individual benefit claims, disability allowances, worker's comp. (N=81)	28.4	37.0	34.6
Enforcement proceedings (civil rights, unfair trade, labor relations, safety, etc.) (N=81)	27.2	54.3	18.5
Other (See Appendix B) (N=40)	55.0	35.0	10.0

Table 6-7
**Patterns in Types of Cases Heard Frequently
by Central Panel ALJ Respondents***

One one type of case heard	
Licensing only (N=26)	35.6%
Ratemaking only (N=1)	1.4
Rulemaking only (N=0)	0.0
Enforcement only (N=1)	1.4
Benefits only (N=8)	11.0
Total	49.4%
Multiple types of cases heard	
Licensing & ratemaking (N=5)	6.8
Licensing & rulemaking (N=3)	4.1
Licensing & enforcement (N=7)	9.6
Licensing & benefits (N=5)**	6.8
Ratemaking & benefits (N=1)**	1.4
Enforcement & benefits (N=2)**	2.7
Licensing & ratemaking & enforcement (N=1)	1.4
Licensing & rulemaking & enforcement (N=4)	5.5
Licensing & enforcement & benefits (N=5)**	6.8
Licensing & ratemaking & rulemaking & enforcement (N=2)	2.7
Licensing & ratemaking & enforcement & benefits (N=1)**	1.4
Licensing & ratemaking & rulemaking & enforcement & benefits (N=1)**	1.4
Total	50.6%

*Respondents in mail questionnaire survey reported hearing these cases frequently. The question asked was: "How often do you preside over each of the following general categories of proceedings?"
**Denotes combination of cases heard which includes regulatory and benefits adjudication. See text for discussion.

Table 6-8
Hearing-Related Reported Activities of Central Panel ALJs

Activities	Frequently	In some cases	Never
Conduct prehearing conferences (N=87)	31.0%	63.2%	5.7%
Direct counsel to brief certain legal issues (N=87)	24.1	75.9	0.0
Go off the record to deal with procedural problems (N=84)	17.9	73.8	8.3
Question witnesses directly (N=87)	55.2	44.8	0.0
Call in witnesses on your own initiative (N=87)	0.0	25.3	74.7
Admit evidence for whatever it may be worth (N=86)	13.9	57.0	29.1
Deliver decisions orally (N=87)	0.0	25.3	74.7
Rule on requests for discovery (N=87)	18.3	63.2	18.4
Employ sanctions for improper conduct in hearing room (N=87)	0.0	32.2	67.8

Table 6-9

Hearing Process: Form of the Administrative Law Judge Decision

California	In writing. It shall contain findings of fact, a determination of the issues presented, and the penalty, if any.
Colorado	In writing. It shall contain findings of fact, conclusions of law, and a recommendation.
Florida	In writing. It shall contain conclusions of law, findings of fact, recommended order, and a preamble with notes of when the hearing was held, who the hearing officer was, etc.
Massachusetts	In writing. The positions shall be identified at the outset. An extensive summary of the evidence is included. Then, there are findings of fact and a conclusion which would involve the untimate finding of fact and the application of the appropriate law to it.
Minnesota	In writing. It shall contain findings of fact, conclusions and recommendations. In rulemaking hearings, in addition to the above, a discussion of the extent to which the agency has established its statutory authority to take the proposed action, and the extent to which the agency has made an affirmative presentation of facts regarding its case. Compensation judges' decsions contain findings of fact, conclusions of law and an award on each issue presented.
Tennessee	In writing. It shall contain findings of fact, conclusions of law, and reasons for the ultimate decision. Findings of fact, if set forth in statutory language, shall be accompanied by a concise and explicit statement of the underlying facts supporting the findings.

Source: Interviews with directors of central panel systems, September-October, 1980.

Table 6-10
Hearing Process: Can Litigant See the ALJ's Decision Before the Agency Issues its Final Order?

California	Yes; After the agency issues its decision, a respondent may petition for reconsideration (Cal. Gov't Code §11521) or seek judicial review (Cal. Gov't Code §11523).
Colorado	Yes; litigant may file exceptions and present arguments before final decision is made.
Florida	Yes; litigant has 10 days to file exceptions.
Massachusetts	Yes; litigant has 14 days to file written exceptions.
Minnesota	Yes; litigant is allowed 10 days to file exceptions and present arguments before a final decision is made.
New Jersey	Yes; litigants have an "exception filing period." (N.J. Stat. Ann. §52:14B-10).
Tennessee	Yes; litigant has ten days to file exceptions. (Tenn. Code Ann. §4-5-315).

Table 6-11
Hearing Process: Is ALJ Decision Final or Recommended?

California	Recommended
Colorado	Recommended (Social service decisions are final)
Florida	Recommended (Final when ALJ decisions involve review of the validity of rules. Also final in adjudicative proceedings if authority is delegated.)
Massachusetts	Recommended (Appeals from Rate Setting Commission are final)
Minnesota	Recommended (Final in workers' compensation cases; occupational safety and health cases; state employee disciplinary matters; discrimination cases under the state Human Rights Law)
New Jersey	Recommended (Decision becomes final if agency does not act within 45 days).
Tennessee	Recommended (Decisions on procedural questions of law are final).

Table 6-12
Hearing Process: The Extent to Which Agencies Accept ALJ Decisions

California	95 per cent accepted as written
Colorado	60 per cent accepted as written, 40 per cent accepted with modifications.
Florida	50-60 per cent accepted as written, 20-30 per cent accepted with modifications.
Massachusetts	85-90 per cent accepted as written, 5-8 per cent accepted with modifications.
Minnesota	75 per cent accepted as written, 15-20 per cent accepted with modifications.
New Jersey	85-90 per cent accepted as written.
Tennessee	High percentage accepted as written.

Source: Interviews with directors of central panel systems, September-October 1980.

Table 6-13
Central Panel Agencies: How Are ALJ Decisions Cataloged?

California	Compiled in the Office of Administrative Hearings and stored by agency.
Colorado	Compiled and stored by each agency.
Florida	Compilation and indexing of all final orders in adjudicative cases.
Massachusetts	Division of Hearing Officers required to compile and index all decisions. (Only rate setting cases are available to the public.)
Minnesota	ALJ and agency decisions on file in the Office of Administrative Hearings. Cataloging system and computerized retrieval system now being constructed.
New Jersey	Office of Administrative Law publishes official reports of ALJ and agency decisions.
Tennessee	Significant decisions of law are indexed to serve as in-house reporting system.

NOTES

1. Interview with director of California central panel, September 1980.
2. *Id.*
3. Interview with director of New Jersey central panel, September 1980.
4. Interview with Chief Hear Examiner in Minnesota, September 1980.
5. Interview with director of Tennessee central panel, September 1980.
6. Interview with Chief Hearing Examiner in Minnesota, September 1980.
7. *Id.*
8. Interview with director of Tennessee central panel, September 1980.
9. Interview with director of Massachusetts central panel, September 1980.
10. Interview with director of Florida central panel, September 1980.

7
Summary and Conclusion

Administrative law judges have become major figures in America's justice system today, though they are so little known that they are sometimes called "the hidden judiciary." When administrative agencies were first established to regulate major industries and to administer government benefit programs, they employed hearing officers to merely assist them in their duties. Since then, the evolution toward judicialized adjudication has resulted in a corps of federal and state ALJs that now resemble judges in their duties as finders of fact or as decisionmakers or both.

But judicialization of administrative adjudication with its focus on providing justice in a new forum has collided with an emerging emphasis on expedient resolution of cases involving administrative agencies. Attempts to resolve this conflict have resulted in new ways in which ALJs are utilized in federal and state governments. Seven states (and now an eighth state) have initiated a new approach to administrative adjudication by placing ALJs in an independent agency—a central pool or central panel.

Creating Central Panels
Each of the panels was created through the action of the state legislature, which established the broad duties and limits of the central panel. The legislative battles associated with this process often helped shape the organizational structures as well as define the central panels' jurisdiction.

These legislative debates spawned a competition among special interests that are critical to the conflict surrounding the central panel notion. That is to say, some agency officials saw in the legislative debates an attempt to replace their administrative authority with the inflexible rule of law, thereby reducing the effectiveness of the system. Proponents of the legislation saw separating ALJs from agencies as a way to improve the administration of justice and to enhance the job status of ALJs. The conflict between law and administrative authority had an impact on personal interests that resulted in fierce agency opposition in the majority of central panel states.

Budgetary Considerations

Under central panel systems, either the agencies or the central panel directors need to make accurate forecasts of requirements for hearings so that realistic budget appropriations can be made. Existing operations are funded through general funding (in which the state legislature appropriates to the central panel a specific sum), revolving fund (in which state legislatures give agencies funds to pay for hearings and the central panel office bills the agencies for the use of ALJs), or a combination of the two. However, we found strikingly little data exists concerning budgetary issues. Most views on the best way to fund central panels are not based on financial studies; necessary data are often unavailable.

Differing Jurisdictions

The central panel approaches share the notion of separating ALJs from agencies but vary in terms of daily operating procedures—from the number of ALJs in each pool to the number of agencies which utilize central panel ALJs. The number of ALJs ranges from five to 45 and not only do states differ in terms of the number of agencies actually utilizing central panel ALJs, there is another distinction based on whether specified agencies must use these ALJs (mandatory jurisdiction) or may use central panel ALJs (permissive jurisdiction).

The Panel Director's Impact

In each of the seven states, the director has shaped the structure of the central panels. While such aspects as organizational structure, jurisdiction, and types of funding may differ, all panels have a director whose role is quite powerful. Directors develop budgets and serve as general office manager. They assign cases to the ALJs, and in many of the states their evaluation of ALJ performance helps determine salary increases. They are also integrally involved in the ALJ selection process in all seven states.

The importance of the position, though, raises a potentially troubling issue. Although the central panel is supposed to eliminate bias, directors are selected by state government officials and could be susceptible to their influence. The newness of the systems and lack of information about the systems preclude any conclusions as to this matter. Current directors downplay this possibility, though, and in a May 1981 workshop on central panels (sponsored by the American Judicature Society and the Administrative Conference of the U.S.), several of them saw their role as a buffer between state government and the decisionmaking independence of ALJs. For example, a director familiar with and accepted by the political system can better resist attempts by a governor to interfere with the administrative process.

84

Role of the ALJ: The Need for Expertise
The ALJ role has often been generally defined in terms of the required amounts of expertise and requisite amounts of independence. Should administrative judges be "generalists," capable of hearing a variety of case types, or "specialists," possessing narrow expertise and only hearing cases in that area?

The need for expertise probably depends on the type of case—a rate-making proceeding may require more technical expertise than a case involving eligibility for benefits. Central panel ALJs preside over a variety of cases, which confuses the issue even more. The respondents to our mail survey of central panel ALJs were nearly evenly split between those who agree and those who disagree that ALJs should have specific expertise. The responses vary substantially by state, suggesting that ALJ viewpoints are fashioned on individual experiences. These experiences include the importance of specialized expertise in the ways directors assign ALJs to their cases.

The Role of the ALJ: The Need for Independence
In both state and federal systems, ALJ independence is related to ALJ performance evaluation. Opponents of ALJ performance evaluation view it as undermining the decisionmaking independence that the central panel approach is supposed to bring about. Proponents of the evaluation of ALJs claim that administrative judges should be accountable for their actions, and accountability, in their view, can come through evaluation. We asked central panel ALJs whether the presence of a performance evaluation system would jeopardize their independence. Although there is fairly uniform opposition to performance evaluation on the part of federal ALJs, this is not necessarily the case among central panel ALJs in our seven states. There were fewer of those central panel ALJs who agreed that performance evaluation would jeopardize their independence than those who disagreed. As with the outcome to our question concerning expertise, the results varied substantially by state. This suggests that the state ALJ viewpoints toward performance evaluation and independence, like their viewpoints on the expertise issue, are fashioned by individual experiences.

The ALJ in the Hearing Process
Central panel ALJs hear a variety of cases. Over half of our respondents report that they hear at least two types of cases frequently. Approximately a fifth of reporting ALJs say the combination of cases they hear includes both regulatory and benefits adjudication—two very different areas of adjudication.

The variety of cases coupled with the physical separation of central panel ALJs from the agencies has led some commentators to question whether those ALJs can acquire the agency guidance they need as to the meaning of agency policies. Directors report that their ALJs will be bound by public agency regulations but not by interpretations of regulations issued by the agencies. Yet agency policies, even when promulgated through the rulemaking function, leave a large amount of room for interpretation. To the extent that the clarity of agency policies varies from type of case to type of case, the ALJ role will differ as well.

Conclusion

The goal of the central panel approach is to promote more objective and efficient adjudication by separating ALJs from the agencies they serve. Our purpose was to focus on the variety of systems encompassed by the central panel notion. We broadly conclude that existing central panels are very different in terms of such dimensions as jurisdiction and the role of both directors of these panels and central panel administrative law judges. As a result of these differences, we found that the role of an ALJ varies from system to system since the discretion and the independence of ALJs are defined in part by what they do on a day-to-day basis.

The central panel approach is an increasingly used concept to balance the need for administrative justice with the goal of efficient and effective administrative action. The way in which this approach is used varies from state to state. These systems differ in factors ranging from means of funding to the number of ALJs to the types of agencies they serve. As a result, the role of the ALJ differs as well. Directors are often extremely influential in shaping the panels but they have different powers and, in addition, profess various operating philosophies about such factors as the importance of specialized expertise when ALJs are assigned to cases.

Finally, the procedures agencies follow in the administrative process also affect central panel operations. One example is the clarity with which agencies make known their policies, including the amount of leeway left by the agencies for interpretation. The duties of the ALJ are affected by these types of agency choices, particularly for central panel ALJs, who must deal with numerous agencies.

The central panel approach, in sum, has provided only the framework for separating ALJs from the agencies. The states have individually adapted the panels' operating procedures to the larger political and economic environments. The result has been seven central panel systems that differ along important dimensions. This flexibility is an important characteristic that the federal government and any state interested in implementing the central panel approach should recognize.

Appendices

Appendix A
Breakdown of Mean Responses by State of Employment

	Calif.	Colo.	Fla.	Mass.	Minn.	N.J.	Tenn.	Aver.
1. How often do you preside over each of the following general categories of proceedings? (0) Infrequently or never (1) Occasionally (2) Frequently								
Licensing	2.000	1.200	2.000	0.875	1.909	1.708	2.000	1.709
Ratemaking	0.053	0.400	0.700	1.286	0.700	0.696	0.000	0.543
Rulemaking	0.167	0.111	1.000	0.833	1.455	0.083	0.000	0.462
Individual benefits	1.150	1.800	0.000	1.625	0.000	0.957	0.000	0.938
Enforcement	1.000	1.100	1.300	1.143	1.300	0.955	1.000	1.086
2. How frequently do you do the following? (0) Never (1) In some cases (2) In most cases (3) In all cases								
Conduct pre-hearing conferences?	0.810	1.100	1.200	1.444	1.545	1.625	1.000	1.276
Rule on discovery requests?	0.381	1.100	2.000	0.889	1.273	1.208	1.000	1.057
Direct counsel to brief issues?	1.000	1.100	1.500	1.333	1.364	1.417	1.000	1.264
Initiate motions?	0.238	0.300	0.500	0.778	0.364	0.833	1.000	0.529
Go off record for procedural problems?	0.950	1.222	0.889	1.333	0.909	1.250	1.500	1.107
Question witnesses directly	1.524	2.000	1.500	1.778	1.545	1.750	1.500	1.667
Call in witnesses on your own?	0.143	0.400	0.100	0.111	0.364	0.333	0.500	0.253
Raise objections during hearings?	0.905	0.600	0.800	0.889	0.636	0.667	1.000	0.759
Admit evidence "for what it's worth?	0.667	1.000	0.500	1.000	0.909	1.083	1.000	0.872
Deliver decisions orally?	0.048	0.800	0.200	0.111	0.182	0.292	0.500	0.253
Sanction improper conduct?	0.238	0.400	0.400	0.111	0.273	0.417	0.500	0.322

	Calif.	Colo.	Fla.	Mass.	Minn.	N.J.	Tenn.	Aver.
3. Do you do any of the following things? (0) Infrequently or never (1) Occasionally (2) Frequently								
Read decisions of other ALJs?	1.143	1.400	1.500	1.444	1.909	1.542	1.000	1.448
Read agency decisions?	1.100	1.800	1.900	1.667	1.727	1.833	1.500	1.628
Read federal court decisions?	0.857	1.200	1.300	1.111	1.364	1.083	1.500	1.115
Read industry publications?	0.619	0.600	0.500	0.500	0.900	0.375	0.000	0.541
Consult others before hearings?	1.190	1.300	1.500	1.375	1.364	1.208	1.500	1.291
Consult others during hearings?	0.571	1.200	1.200	1.333	1.200	0.917	1.500	0.988
Request decision drafts from clerk?	0.000	0.222	0.000	1.000	0.545	0.391	0.500	0.333
Talk with the private bar?	0.238	0.800	0.500	0.889	1.000	0.292	1.000	0.529
Make policy suggestions to agencies?	0.190	1.000	0.700	0.667	0.636	0.250	1.000	0.483
Make procedure suggestions to agencies?	0.333	1.100	0.700	0.778	0.545	0.375	1.000	0.563
Disqualify yourself?	0.286	0.500	0.000	0.125	0.182	0.548	0.000	0.291
Attend professional Seminars?	0.905	1.200	1.000	0.889	1.182	1.292	1.000	1.092
4. How much of the total time spent doing your job is devoted to the following activities? (all answers are percentages)								
a. Pre-trial preparation	8.286	7.800	10.600	7.556	13.182	9.708	5.000	9.356
b. Pre-hearing negotiations	1.333	5.300	6.300	10.000	6.182	10.500	7.500	6.540
c. Presiding at hearings	44.190	30.800	25.700	27.778	22.273	28.250	45.000	31.678
d. Writing decisions	28.571	36.300	33.800	43.333	38.364	32.000	30.000	33.805
e. Travelling	8.619	5.700	10.700	1.111	5.909	5.625	5.000	6.494
f. Administrative duties	6.810	10.400	6.400	9.667	12.182	12.792	6.500	9.793
g. Other hearing duties	2.190	3.700	6.500	1.111	1.909	1.125	1.000	2.391

90

	Calif.	Colo.	Fla.	Mass.	Minn.	N.J.	Tenn.	Aver.
5. Are you assigned to hear cases of only one agency? (0) No (1) Yes	0.000	0.200	0.000	0.222	0.091	0.043	0.000	0.071
6. How many cases per month do you have pending before you?	18.750	52.100	22.000	11.000	7.182	27.957	17.500	23.345
7. How many cases do you decide after a formal hearing each month?	15.350	35.700	11.600	5.875	14.696	9.500	14.762	
8. To what extent do you agree or disagree with the following statements? (0) Strongly Disagree (1) Disagree (2) Undecided (3) Agree (4) Strongly agree								
An ALJ should be free to deviate from CP rules of procedure if the situation necessitates.	3.000	3.000	2.700	2.000	2.000	2.625	3.000	2.628
Developing the record of a case is one of the most important tasks of an ALJ.	3.571	3.444	3.000	3.444	3.636	3.625	2.000	3.465
An ALJ should intervene more in a case where one of the litigants is not represented by counsel.	3.095	3.500	2.778	3.333	3.182	3.083	3.500	3.151
An ALJ should have specific expertise in the areas over which he/she presides.	1.000	2.700	1.700	3.000	2.909	2.500	1.000	2.138
An ALJ should adhere to established agency policy when deciding a case.	2.571	2.600	2.111	2.875	2.273	2.667	3.000	2.553
Most agency rules and regulations are clear enough to be effectively applied to individual cases.	2.524	1.889	2.111	2.333	2.182	2.583	1.500	2.341
ALJs are adequately compensated.	1.714	1.000	1.200	0.222	0.727	1.174	0.000	1.105

	Calif.	Colo.	Fla.	Mass.	Minn.	N.J.	Tenn.	Aver.
ALJs are more effective with a central panel system.	3.333	3.000	3.600	3.500	3.364	3.000	3.500	3.259
ALJs in central panel systems experience too much variety in cases coming before them.	0.476	0.800	0.500	0.889	1.182	1.174	1.000	0.849
ALJs are under undue pressure to decide cases quickly.	2.143	2.300	2.000	1.778	2.727	2.478	2.000	2.267
Agency oficials still view ALJs as agency employees.	2.048	2.000	1.444	2.667	1.000	1.708	1.500	1.802
CP systems better insulate ALJs from inappropriate agency influence.	3.476	3.500	3.800	3.500	2.818	3.391	3.500	3.412
CP ALJs will be more subject to inappropriate agency influence if their offices are located within an agency.	3.476	3.400	3.300	3.000	2.364	3.130	2.500	3.023
Mechanism for the evaluation of overall ALJ performance will undermine the independence of ALJs.	1.619	1.800	3.000	1.714	1.909	1.478	1.500	1.810
Mechanisms for the evaluation of quantitative ALJ performance will undermine the independence of ALJs.	2.048	2.000	3.100	2.000	2.000	1.913	2.000	2.118
CP system ensures ALJ independence.	3.810	3.200	4.000	4.000	2.909	3.667	4.000	3.628

9. To what extent do any of the following problems arise in your work?
(0) Not a problem
(1) Somewhat a problem
(2) Significant problem

	Calif.	Colo.	Fla.	Mass.	Minn.	N.J.	Tenn.	Aver.
Delay in proceedings.	1.000	1.800	1.200	0.889	0.636	0.625	1.000	0.954
Ambiguity in law.	0.619	0.800	0.500	0.667	0.818	0.417	0.500	0.598
Too great a caseload.	0.476	1.500	0.400	0.444	0.545	1.042	0.000	0.736
Cases overly complex.	0.095	0.300	0.100	0.000	0.727	0.500	0.500	0.310

	Calif.	Colo.	Fla.	Mass.	Minn.	N.J.	Tenn.	Aver.
Lack of agency policy enunciation.	0.238	0.400	0.000	0.222	0.300	0.375	0.500	0.279
Lack of review standards.	0.524	0.000	0.300	0.333	0.909	0.875	0.000	0.552
Review by unqualified persons.	0.550	0.600	0.667	0.222	0.727	0.917	0.000	0.647
Lack of procedural uniformity.	0.286	0.900	0.600	0.333	0.182	0.625	0.000	0.471
Too close supervision.	0.143	0.100	0.100	0.000	0.091	0.125	0.000	0.103
10. What is your age? (All answers are mean years)	51.500	46.000	43.700	33.667	36.182	42.792	32.000	43.244
11. Are you an attorney?	1.000	1.000	1.000	1.000	1.000	0.696	1.000	0.918
12. Type of law school attended? (1) Private (2) Public	1.571	1.600	1.500	1.000	1.700	1.625	1.500	1.526

Appendix B
"Other" Types of Cases Reported Heard by Central Panel ALJs

Civil Service (employment protections)

Civil Service disciplinary actions

Social Service privileges, teacher tenure, parole violations

OSHA, securities matters, agricultural laws, motor vehicle registration, education matters, veterans rights, some tax related hearings, et al.

Teacher dismissal hearing, local government personnel hearings

Rule challenges

Confiscation for drug offenses

Environmental permits variances

State contract disputes and teacher layoff proceedings and personel disciplinary hearings

Education Appeals

Civil Service

Medical reimbursement cases

Appeals from agency denials

Tax, environmental

Teacher tenure and related job issues

Hearings on continued involuntary placement in state mental hospitals and refusal of patients to take prescribed medication

Personnel disciplinary hearings

Establishment of watershed districts or projects; special education placement, data privacy

Forfeiture

Welfare, public assistance, juvenile parole

Airport noise hearing

Institutional claims

Taxation, rule challenges

Teacher dismissals and layoffs

Educational employees—layoffs, probationary dismissals, firings, etc.

Retirement hearings

Educational disputes

Sale of agricultural products (under bond)

Education law hearings

Bibliography

Abrams, Norman. "Administrative Law Judge Systems: The California View," 29 *Admin. L. Rev.* 487 (1977).

Aronsohn, Richard F. "Unique Remedy for Traditional Problems," No. 92 *New Jersey Lawyer* 38 (1980).

Baum, Laurence. "Judicial Specialization, Litigant Influence, and Substantive Policy: The Court of Customs and Patent Appeals," 11 *Law and Soc. Rev.* 823 (1977).

Bobby, Charles H. "An Introduction to Practice and Procedure Under The California Administrative Procedure Act," 15 *The Hastings L. J.* 258 (1964).

Brudno, Barbara. "Fairness and Bureaucracy: The Demise of Procedural Due Process for Welfare Claimants," 25 *The Hastings L. J.* 813 (1974).

Cary, William L. "Why I Oppose The Divorce of The Judicial Function From Federal Regulatory Agencies," 51 *A.B.A.J.* 33 (1965).

Clarkson, John G. "The History of The California Administrative Procedure Act," 15 *The Hastings L. J.* 237 (1964).

Coan, George R. "Operational Aspects of a Central Hearing Examiners Pool: California's Experiences," 3 *Florida State Univ. L. Rev.* 86 (1975).

Cooper, Frank E. *State Administrative Law* (Volumes 1 and 2). New York: Bobbs-Merrill, 1965.

Davis, Frederick. "Judicialization of Administrative Law: The Trial-Type Hearing and The Changing Status of The Hearing Officer," 1977 *Duke L. J.* 389 (1977).

Dietz, Henry A. "Local Adaptation of the California Administrative Procedure Act—A Plea For Research and Study," 15 *The Hastings L. J.* 310 (1964).

Freedman, James O. *Crisis and Legitimacy.* Cambridge University Press, 1978.

Grau, Charles W. "The Limits of Planned Change In The Courts." 6/1 *The Just. Sys. J.* 84 (1981).

Harves, Duane. "Making administrative proceedings more efficient and effective: how the ALJ central panel system works in Minnesota," 65

Judicature 257 (Nov. 1981); "Independent Hearing Examiners—The Minnesota Experience," 49 *The Hennepin Lawyer* 6 (1980).

Hazard, Geoffrey C., Jr. "The Tennessee Administrative Procedures Act: An Outsider's Perspective," 6 *Memphis State Univ. L. Rev.* 143 (1976).

Hector, Louis J. "Problems of the CAB and The Independent Regulatory Commissions," 69 *Yale L. J.* 931 (1960).

Heflin, Howell, Chairman. Hearings before the Subcommittee for Consumers of the Committee on Commerce, Science and Transportation. United State Senate (Sept. 4-5, 1980).

Kestin, Howard H. "Reform of The Administrative Process," No. 92 *New Jersey Lawyer* 35 (1980).

Kochman, Carl. "Part II, The Role of The Hearing Officer—A Private Practitioner's Point of View," 44 *California L. Rev.* 212 (1956).

Lakusta, Boris H. "Operations In An Agency Not Subject To The APA: Public Utilities Commission," 44 *California L. Rev.* 218 (1956).

Levinson, L. Harold. "The central panel system: a framework that separates ALJs from administrative agencies," 65 *Judicature* 236 (Nov. 1981); "Contested Cases Under The Tennessee Uniform Administrative Procedures Act," 6 *Memphis State Univ. L. Rev.* 215 (1976); "Elements of The Administrative Process: Formal, Semi-Formal, and Free-Form Models," 26 *The American Univ. L. Rev.* 872 (1977); "The Florida APA: 1974 Revision and 1975 Amendments," 29 *University of Miami L. Rev.* 617 (1975).

"Logan-Walter Bill Fails," 27 *A.B.A.J.* 52 (Jan. 1941).

Lubbers, Jeffrey S. "Federal Administrative Law Judges: A Focus On Our Invisible Judiciary." 33 *Admin. L. Rev.* No. 1 (Winter, 1981); "A unified corps of ALJs: a proposal to test the idea at the federal level," 65 *Judicature* 266 (Nov. 1981).

Macy, John W., Jr. "The APA and The Hearing Examiner: Products of A Viable Political Society," 27 *Fed. B. J.* 351 (1967).

Mans, Thomas C. "Selecting The 'Hidden Judiciary': How The Merit Process Works In Choosing Administrative Law Judges (Part I)," 63 *Judicature* 60 (Aug. 1979); "Selecting The 'Hidden Judiciary': How The Merit Process Works In Choosing Administrative Law Judges (Part II)," 63 *Judicature* 130 (Sept. 1979).

McQuade, John J., Jr. "The Central Panel Approach To Administrative Adjudication: The Massachusetts Division of Hearing Officers," 10 *The Advocate, The Suffolk Univ. L. School J.* 14 (1978).

Mashaw, Jerry L., et. al. *Social Security Hearings and Appeals.* D. C. Heath, 1978.

Musolf, Lloyd D. "Independent Hearing Officers: The California Experiments," 14 *The Western Pol. Q.* 195 (1961).

Nathanson, Nathanial L. "Social Science, Administrative Law, and The

Information Act of 1966," 21 *Social Problems* 21 (1973).

Nonet, Philippe. *Administrative Justice, Advocacy and Change In A Government Agency.* New York Russell Sage Foundation, 1969.

Note: "A Survey of Principal Procedural Elements Among State Administrative Procedure Acts," 22 *Cleveland State L. Rev.* 281 (1973).

Office of Administrative Hearings—Report To The Governor and To The Legislature of California. State of California, Department of General Services, 1979.

Pfeiffer, Paul N. "Hearing Cases Before Several Agencies—Odyssey of an Administrative Law Judge," 27 *Admin. L. Rev.* 217 (1975).

Pops, Gerald M. "The Judicialization of Federal Administrative Law Judges: Implications For Policymaking," 81 *West Virginia L. Rev.* 169 (1979).

Pound, Roscoe. *Jurisprudence* (Vol. II). St. Paul: West Publishing Co., 1959.

"The Quest For Justice In Maine Administrative Procedure: The Administrative Code In Application and Theory," 18 *Maine L. Rev.* 218 (1966).

Reich, Charles A. "The New Property," 73 *The Yale L. J.* 733 (1964); "Individual Rights and Social Welfare: The Emerging Legal Issues," 74 *The Yale L. J.* 1245 (1965).

Report of the Committee on the Study of the Utilization of Administrative Law Judges (LaMacchia Committee Report), U.S. Civil Service Comm'n (July 30, 1974).

Report by The Comptroller General of the United States. "Management Improvements in the Administrative Process: Much Remains to be Done (1979).

Riccio, Ronald J. "Due Process in Quasi-Judicial Administrative Hearings: Confining The Examiner To One Hat," 2 *Seaton Hall L. J.* 398 (1971).

Rich, Malcolm, "Adapting the central panel system: a study of seven states," 65 *Judicature* 246 (Nov. 1981).

Rosenblum, Victor G. "Evaluation of Administrative Law Judges: Aspects of Purpose, Policy and Feasibility." Draft submitted to Administrative Conference of the U.S., Feb. 1981 (cited with permission of author); *The Administrative Law Judge in the Administrative Process: Interrelations of Case Law with Statutory and Pragmatic Factors in Determining ALJ Roles,* printed in Subcomm. on Social Security of the House Comm. on Ways and Means, 94th Cong., 1st Sess., Recent Studies Relevant to the Disability Hearings and Appeals Crisis, 171-245 (Comm. Print December 20, 1975).

Ruhlen, Merritt. "Manual For Administrative Law Judges" (Administrative Conference of the United States, 1974).

Russell, Harold L., "State Administrative Law—1978 Today and Tomorrow," Presentation before the sections of Administrative Law, Local

Government Law and Public Utility Law, New York, August 8, 1978.

Scalia, Antonin. "The Hearing Examiner Loan Program," 1971 *Duke L. J.* 319 (1971); "The ALJ Fiasco—A Reprise," 47 *The Univ. of Chicago L. Rev.* 57 (1979).

Sharon, Amiel T. "The Measure of an Administrative Law Judge," 19/4 *The Judges' J.* 20 (1980).

Sharp, Sally B. "State Administrative Procedure—A Selective Bibliography," 6 *Memphis State Univ. L. Rev.* 325 (1976).

Shields, Stephen L. "The Tennessee Uniform Administrative Procedures Act: Procedure Before Hearing," 6 *Memphis State Univ. L. Rev.* 201 (1976).

Starr, C. M (Bud) II. "The California Legislature Tries To Curb Bureaucratic Regulations and Expand Judicial Review," 7 *Orange County B. Assoc. J.* 120 (1980); "California's New Office of Administrative Law and Other Amendments to the California APA: A Bureau to Curb Bureaucracy and Judicial Review, Too," 32 *Admin. L. Rev.* 713 (1980).

State of California Department of Finance, Program Evaluation Unit. "Centralized U.S. Decentralized Services, Phase II, Administrative Hearings," (1977).

Tenbroek, Jacobus "Operations Partially Subject To The APA Public Welfare Administration," 44 *California L. Rev.* 242 (1956).

Testimony of William Fauver, Before the Senate Committee on Governmental Affairs, 96th Cong., 1st Sess. (May 1979).

Testimony of William Fauver, Hearings on Administrative Law Judge System Before the Subcommittee of the Senate Commitee on Commerce, Science, and Transportation, 96th Cong., 2nd Sess. 28 (Sept. 4-5, 1980).

Weiss, Steven G. "Comparison of Practice Before the OAL and Before Agencies," No. 92 *New Jersey Lawyer* 43 (1980).

Zwerdling, Joseph. "Reflections On The Role of An Administrative Judge," 25 *Admin. L. Rev.* 9 (1973).

About the authors

Malcolm C. Rich is a 1979 graduate of the Northwestern University School of Law where he was the recipient of the Northwestern University Center for Urban Affairs and Policy Research fellowship.

He is a practicing attorney with the Chicago law firm of Canel, Aronson & Whitted and a research investigator for the Chicago Council of Lawyers. He formerly was a research attorney with the American Judicature Society.

Wayne Eli Brucar graduated from Loyola University of Chicago in 1975 with a B.A., Cum Laude, in communications and psychology, and received a J.D., with High Honors, from IIT/Chicago-Kent College of Law in 1981. He is currently a hearing officer with the Illinois Commerce Commission.